FACE VALUES

How to read people and adjust your presentation to connect with them in less than three minutes

Pamela Holloway & Michael Lovas

(c) 2000 AboutPeople

Face Values

Copyright © 2000
AboutPeople

All rights reserved.
No part of this book may be reproduced in any form or by any means without permission in writing from the authors.

First printing 2000
Second printing 2005
Third printing 2008

Face Values™ is a trademarked methodology and is the sole property of Michael Lovas, Pam Holloway and AboutPeople.

About People
www.aboutpeople.com

Table of Contents

Introduction 7
Reading Faces 9
    What to look for in a person's face 13
    Overview of the Four People Type "Colors" 19
    How it Applies 28
    Reading Children 31
    What if you can't See the Person's Face? 34
    Other Facial Elements to Consider 36

The Face Values Program 39
    How Face Values Maps to Other Programs 40
    Other Ways to Identify People Types 41

Individual People Types 49
    GREEN - The Analytical 50
    BLUE - The Amiable 65
    RED - The Expressive 79
    GOLD - The Driver 91
    Practice: Presenting to each of the Four Types 105
    Combinations - People Who are a Blend of Types ... 111
    Putting Your Knowledge to Work 122

Face Values Matrix 127

Part II - Identifying Mental Filters 155
    Procedures and Options 165
    Proactive and Reactive 173
    Time, Improvement and Change 183
    Internal and External 189
    Sort Preference 195
    Criteria: What's important to you? 201
    Inclusion or Exclusion 205
    Questions 211
    Mental Filters Matrix 217

aboutpeople.com

INTRODUCTION

We knew there was a link between the lines on a person's face and his or her personality type. We explored phrenology and the Chinese approach to face reading. Both took us in the wrong direction. Then, when we were conducting Personality Type seminars, we found it. We simply recognized the similarities in the facial lines of each of the four Personality Types.

Let me explain. The face you make most often etches itself into your skin. Then, after age thirty, that facial expression has become a set of lines that simply shows what face you've made most often over your lifetime. If we can identify the psychology behind that face, we've also identified your values, communication style, decision-making style and Personality Type. That's exactly what Face Values does.

We've taught thousands of people how to use the Face Values methodology and are delighted to see it become even more popular over time.

This book is divided into two primary sections: 1) Reading Faces and 2) Identifying Mental Filters.

In Reading Faces, we describe the six Key Facial Characteristics to look for and the personalities associated with each. We discuss in detail the four primary personality "colors" and give you information on how to present to, manage, and better relate to each one.

In Identifying Mental Filters, we teach you how to recognize mental-filter configurations, which provide you with even more valuable information on the person you're talking with. Mental Filters tell you how he filters information and makes decisions. You can also use them to learn what motivates him, and what confuses him.

Our litmus test for this program is simple - can you use it immediately? We have seen over and over again that the answer is YES!

Reading Faces

Picture yourself standing in front of a potential client. Neither of you says a word. Within seconds, you know things about her that allow you to speak in words and use a delivery style that make it easy for her to begin trusting you very quickly.

And, you learned such important things during a few seconds of silence! What happened? How did you do that? You are about to learn some of those skills.

Is this just another Personality Types program?

That's a common question people ask when they are first introduced to the Face Values program. "Is it a Personality Type program like Myers-Briggs or DISC?"

In a word - No. Face Values is unique in many respects and one of the most important aspects is that it doesn't require a test. DISC and Myers-Briggs and virtually all the programs in use for distinguishing personality characteristics involve a written test. That's not a practical solution in the real world, is it?

Think about it. When you're standing in front of a new client, you can't very well ask him to fill out a questionnaire so that you'll know how to sell your product. *"Excuse me, Mr. Wilson, but could you answer these 64 questions so I'll know how to sell to you."*

We recognized early on in our work that it simply isn't practical to depend on any system that requires a test. You absolutely must be able

IMPROVEMENT NUMBER 1 - FACE VALUES IS TEST-FREE!

to discern personality traits without it. One of the ways you do that is by reading faces.

The map of the face provides great insight into the heart and mind of the person. You just have to know how to read the map. And that's what Face Values enables you to do.

What makes reading faces a valid way to determine someone's psychology?

As students of psychology and practitioners of Neuro-linguistic Programming, we've been fascinated with faces for years.

We wondered why people inherently trust one face over another. And exactly what is it about a face that makes us trust or not trust?

> *"The face is like a treasure map of character, full of invisible and shifting lines, a boon for it's decoder."*
>
> – Daniel McNeill: The Face – A Natural History

We discovered that you can have two people with the same genetics and facial features, who are the same age and have the same stress level, and over time, one will end up with no lines on his face while the other will have a virtual road map of every good and bad experience of their lives. Just look at the two faces on the next page.

What does all this mean and why is it important?

To understand what it means requires better understanding of the face itself. The face is made up of bone, muscle and skin - 44 muscles to be exact, 22 on either side. Like most muscles, the facial muscles are anchored in bone. Unlike most muscles, they attach to the skin.

When we "make a face," so to speak, we exercise certain muscles, which pull the skin a certain way.

Take a minute and make the biggest grin you can. Feel the muscles in your face. Now release the grin and allow the muscles to go back to their natural state. How does this feel different?

Imagine what your face would look like if you wore this grin all the time.

Face Values teaches you how to read the lines on a person's face. Why? Because these lines give you a glimpse into the psyche of the person. They show you how the person spends her time. Thinking, smiling, judging, and amazement produce four very different facial maps and represent four different personality types.

We express our prominent attitude toward life through our facial muscles. Who we are, what we value and how we spend our time causes us to wear a certain look or expression. The more

THE FACE YOU WEAR MOST OFTEN

frequently we wear that look, the deeper are the lines that illustrate it. As we age, attitude carves itself into our skin wrinkles.

When you see someone's wrinkles, you get a great picture of who she really is and what's important to her.

Facial lines illustrate values. And values drive attitude. If I value babies and kittens and loving relationships, the sight of those things will trigger a smile in me. I will look for evidence that supports my love of babies and kittens and loving relationships. So, I will find them often and smile frequently.

After I've smiled for twenty years, I'll have little lines showing my typical facial expression.

Thus, reading facial lines gives you important clues about a person – what they value and how they make decisions.

As a sales professional, would such information be important to you? Absolutely! As face readers, we're simply following evidence to the source.

Now let's continue with details on what to look for in a person's face.

What to look for in a person's face

Face Reading – 6 Key Characteristics

Face Values focuses on six key facial characteristics:

1. Smile lines around the eyes and mouth
2. Short vertical lines between the eyes
3. Horizontal excitement lines across the forehead
4. Lack of lines
5. Judging and anger lines across the forehead
6. Eyes (Piercing, sparkling, distant or loving)

These characteristics correlate to four personality types (we call them People Types.)

They are:

        BLUE   • The Amiable

        GREEN • The Analytical

        RED   • The Expressive

        GOLD   • The Driver

Here's a quick reference for identifying People Types by their facial characteristics:

People Type	Facial Characteristics
Blue	• Smile lines around the eyes and mouth • Warm and friendly eyes
Green	• Short vertical line(s) between the eyes • Distant, "look right through you" gaze
Red	• Horizontal excitement lines across the forehead • Wide open, dancing, mischievous eyes
Gold	• Judging lines across the forehead • Lack of lines • Focused, piercing gaze

Lack of Lines

Look at the person's forehead. If there are no lines there, that indicates the person is not very expressive. A face that tends to be "expressionless" most of the time will produce few lines. This lack of lines is characteristic of the Gold People Type, the always in control Driver.

Judging Lines

Look at the lines above and to the outside of the brow. These are "judging" lines. Picture someone who raises her eyebrows often as if saying, "Oh really?" or "I don't believe you." The lines above and to the outside of the eyes are created by raising eyebrows in a judging stance. This is characteristic of the Gold People Type.

Vertical lines between the eyebrows

Short vertical lines between the eyebrows indicate deep thought. People with those lines take in information – great quantities of information. Their minds are always at work doing what they do best – thinking. The vertical line between the brow is characteristic of the Green People Type – The Analytical.

Roy Rogers Lines

"Roy Rogers" lines are created from excitement. The person who has them has a tendency to get excited and raise both eyebrows as if to say, "Wow!" These horizontal lines are characteristic of the Red People Type – The Expressive.

Smile Lines

Look for those sweet-looking smile lines on the outside of the eyes. They're created when the person smiles in his or her eyes. That's a nurturing smile as in, "Oh look at the baby!" or "You need a hug." Smile lines are characteristic of the Blue People Type – The Amiable.

The Eyes

Facial muscles are one of the telling components used in Face Values. The eyes are another.

The eyes are indeed a window to the soul. Eyes provide insight into the inner person. Think about it. A distant, far away look suggests a person whose head is somewhere else – not quite in the moment – busy thinking about something.

A playful twinkle suggests this is a person who enjoys life, someone who is passionate, involved and creative.

Cold, piercing eyes that seem to be focused on a target suggest a serious driving sort of personality that likes being in control.

You can use the eyes to test your initial assumptions about people.

OVERVIEW OF THE FOUR PEOPLE TYPE "COLORS"

Here are overviews of each of the four People Types or "Colors." Following this overview is a much more in-depth and comprehensive description of each Type or Color.

GREEN – The Analytical

Remember the absent minded professor? That's a typical Green – He is often lost in thought, busy creating a new and better world.

To those around him, the Green can appear cold and aloof, even angry. The Green thinking line or hatchet mark between the eyes is a reflection of how the Green spends his time – thinking, analyzing, solving problems.

Greens are inventive, creative, extremely bright and fiercely independent. They like to take things apart and they can usually put them back together again. They are inquisitive, focused, driven and they have an insatiable appetite for knowledge.

Because they are so mental, Greens sometimes are out of touch with their emotions and have difficulty relating to others on a non-intellectual level. Greens typically have a distant, far away look in their eyes. With the Green, you get the feeling they are looking through you rather than at you.

BLUE – The Amiable

Blues are the polar opposites to Greens. Where Greens are process-oriented, objective, and driven by their heads, Blues are people oriented, subjective and driven by their hearts.

Blues are relaters, peacemakers, and care-givers. They're the people that everyone confides in. They are friends to people, animals, the earth and all things natural.

Blues tend to be traditional, practical, and not prone to risk-taking. They dislike conflict and typically "go with the flow."

Blues are grounded, earthy and realistic. They express their emotions, both happy and sad. They surround themselves with things that make them smile (like kids and puppies) and they smile a lot. The Blue smile produces the Blue smile lines around the eyes and mouth. The eyes of the Blue are warm and loving.

RED – The Expressive

Reds are the most sociable of all the colors and are natural entertainers. They are highly creative and inventive, quick-witted, and able to think on their feet.

They are "out-of-the-box" thinkers who are always coming up with wild and crazy new ideas. They love freedom and hate being controlled.

Reds are natural communicators, networkers, connection-makers and relationship builders.

They are energetic and energized and surround themselves with people and situations that excite and entertain. The tend to develop "Roy Rogers" lines across their forehead as a result of wearing the excitable face for so much of their lives.

Reds have expressive, magical eyes. Remember the phrase "a twinkle in his eye?" That's a Red!

GOLD – The Driver

Golds are get-it-done, bottom-line oriented task masters. They are good at facing an issue or problem head on. They love solving problems. They value stability, orderliness, accuracy and most of all, results.

Golds like structure, following the rules, tradition, consistency. They look for opportunities to be in control, to make things simple and efficient, to achieve immediate results and "tell it like it is."

Because Golds often wear a cool, calm and collected "poker face" with little or no expression, they tend to have fewer facial lines than the other colors.

If Golds have lines, they are typically the judging lines that result from the raised eyebrow (we call this the Judgment Line) or the "V" running from the bridge of the nose up the forehead. Darwin called this the grief line. We call it the Frustration Line.

Golds and Reds sometimes share similar lines across their foreheads. The way to tell the two apart is simply to look at their eyes. Golds have a piercing commanding look, while Reds have more of a fun-loving twinkle.

Here is a quick overview of the general characteristics of each People Type.

Green – The Analytical	**Blue – The Amiable**
• Process-oriented • Intellectual and insightful • A passion for learning and knowledge • Complex problem solver • Analytical, logical • Focused • Curious about how things work • Visionary/Futurist • Needs independence and quiet • Can't relax or feel comfortable unless accomplishing something • Often appears distant & aloof	• People-oriented • Friendly, warm-hearted, emphatic • A passion for helping other people • Peacekeeper, negotiator • Sensitive • Cautious • Concerned with creating a safe and comfortable environment • Dependable • Consistent • Likes social interaction but not the limelight • Compassionate
Red – The Expressive	**Gold – The Driver**
• Self-oriented • Creative and imaginative • Passion for life • Quick-witted and humorous • Good communicator and translator • Strong demand for freedom & variety • Likes dealing with new ideas and concepts • Likes being in the limelight • Questions the status quo • Social, relates well to others • Fun-loving	• Bottom-line oriented • Responsible and accountable • Passion for getting things done • Makes decisions easily • Likes being in control • Competitive • Sets high standards • Likes having a plan and following it • Respects authority, rules and procedures • Excels at time management • Perfectionist

GQ Men of the Year 2000

The GQ Men of the Year 2000 are great examples of different People Types.

Take a look at the picture on the next page and see if you can spot the psychological differences, just by looking:

Which of the three has the excitable raised eyebrows and Roy Rogers lines across his forehead?

Which one is the thinking man with the vertical lines between his eyes?

Which one has a calm, cool, poker face – a lack of distinguishing lines or expression?

Chris Rock is obviously the energetic, excitable Red.

Harrison Ford is the Green Analytical.

George Clooney is a combination of Gold and Blue. He has some blue smile lines around his eyes (which unfortunately you can't see in this picture), but his face is most notable here for its lack of expression, which denotes the Gold People Type.

Face Values 25

Color Variations on "Ready – Aim – Fire"

Here are variations of the phrase "Ready – Aim – Fire" to match each of the Colors.

Red	Fire! Ready - Aim!
Blue	Ready – Aim – Check to see how everyone else feels Fire!
Green	Ready – Aim – Redesign the sights – Ready – Aim – Fine-tune the redesign – Ready – Aim…..
Gold	Get someone else to get ready – Aim – Fire!

COLOR COMBINATIONS

Every person's personality contains all four Types. No one is only one Type, however, many people are dominant in their Type within a specific context or situation.

It will be easier for you to read a person who has a dominant Type because the lines on his or her face will reflect primarily that Type.

A person who displays more than one Type on his face may be a little more difficult to read. The photo to the right shows a man with some of all four types (or at least three of the four). He has the smile lines of the Blue, the Green vertical lines between the eyes, and the Red horizontal excitement lines. He is a combination of several types and in fact is fairly balanced between the three.

Although more difficult to read, those with strong combinations of several types are easier to relate to because they respond to more than one approach and relate well to the other People Types.

Even where there are combinations of lines, a person may still operate in a dominant type within a particular context.

When you encounter a combination personality, read the lines that activate the most when you're talking with that person. That will tell you what People Type or personality is engaged at the time.

How it Applies

Let's do an experiment. Picture four strangers sitting in front of you. Perhaps they're on a benefits review board for a corporation. One person is a corporate attorney. Another is a human resources advisor. The third is a sales rep. And the fourth is a quality control engineer. Do you speak to them in the same way?

1. Does each one plan his financial security the same way?
2. Does each one map his career path in the same way?
3. Is each comfortable with the same amount of risk?
4. Does each one need the same amount of written information?
5. Do they all make decisions at the same speed?

If you answered Yes to any of those questions, think again. Each represents a different People Type. Do you know how to differentiate one from the other?

Now, picture yourself speaking very briefly with each of the four people mentioned above. If you address each person using words and phrases that are comfortable to him, don't you think he'll be more receptive? If you make your presentation relevant to his primary values, you'll have a better shot at building your credibility, establishing rapport and accomplishing your goal.

Within fifteen seconds, you could have a good idea which person is motivated by family values and people relationships; which one is motivated by the bottom-line, numbers and efficiency; which one will base decisions on gut feelings and emotion; and which one will research it to death and then fail to make a decision.

On the other hand, if you don't know the People Type of your prospect, you face overwhelming odds of serious communication blunders without realizing it.

You'll likely force distance between you, and rapport and trust will fade farther and farther away. That's because you might present products or ideas emphasizing benefits or values that he is not interested in. You might use words and language structures that confuse him.

Even if your presentation is perfect, you could easily deliver it inappropriately for that person. In fact, since each People Type represents roughly 25% of the population, until you can recognize each one, you stand a 75% chance of talking to someone who isn't understanding you.

> EACH PEOPLE TYPE REPRESENTS
>
> **25%**
>
> OF THE POPULATION.
>
> IF YOU SPEAK ONLY ONE LANGUAGE, YOU MISS
>
> **75%**
>
> OF YOUR AUDIENCE.

What if the person has no lines?

People often ask us whether you can read the face of a person who has had cosmetic surgery to remove their lines. The answer is Yes.

Here's an example. I am a Green with the classic vertical hatchet mark between my eyes. If I were to deaden that muscle and pull the skin back to remove the wrinkles, the line would go away. I wouldn't be able to make the Analytical's frown even if I wanted to, would I?

Yes and no. Since my personality hasn't changed, I will continue to make that face because I will continue to spend most of my time thinking. The lines may not carve themselves into my face, but I will still make the face.

As professional face readers, you need only pay attention to my reactions and imagine what the face would look like if the muscles had not been altered.

I learned this from watching Oprah Winfrey. I'm guessing Oprah is a combination of Gold, Red and Green but has had a few cosmetic touch-ups here and there to remove the Green Analytical's mark and the Red forehead lines.

Watch how she responds to new information. She has a distant sort of gaze in her eyes and it is as though her face wants to be in Analytical's pose, but just can't quite get there.

Her spontaneity and warmth are Red qualities and are also reflected in her expression. You will occasionally see the Red forehead lines fire when she gets excited.

If you think someone has had cosmetic surgery and you want to check your assumptions, simply look at their eyes. The eyes will help you accurately calibrate their People Type.

READING CHILDREN

In much the same way that you can read a person who has surgically removed the telling lines, you can read a child who has not yet worn his or her expression long enough to have produced the telling lines.

Take a look at these four children and see if you get a sense of their personality. See if you can imagine what their faces will look like in 40 years.

Here's our read of the four children shown on the previous page. The little boy in the top left corner is a Gold. Even at his young age, he is serious and his face is very commanding. The little boy next to him is Red – you can tell he likes to have fun. The little boy in the second row is Green – a serious look like the Gold, but a bit distant. You get the sense his head is somewhere else. The little girl is a Blue. Look at her eyes – there is a warmth and sweetness there.

How about these four teenagers?

The teenage girl in the top left is Blue. Even at a young age, you can already see the smile lines around her eyes. The girl on the top right is Gold – serious and focused in her expression. The boy on the bottom left is Green. He has the Green "look right through you" look. The boy on the right is Red. His eyes are wide open and his brows are raised. He's looking for the humor in the situation.

Remember, young people do not have facial lines, yet. But they do make facial expressions. The expressions a teenager makes repeatedly will etch themselves in her skin after about age thirty. However, before age thirty, you can still see what her People Type is, just by paying attention to the facial expressions she makes.

For example, look at the girl at the top left. She's wearing a nice big, comfortable smile. It's a genuine, smile, but, her eyebrows are not raised. That tells you she is not a Red. It's a comfortable, engaged smile. That tells you she's likely not Green.

WHAT IF YOU CAN'T SEE THE PERSON'S FACE?

An obvious question we often get is "What if you can't see the other person's face? Can you use Face Values over the phone? The answer is Yes. A primary element of the Face Values program is the connection between language and behavior. You listen to the words people use and pay attention to behavior (yes you can get behavioral clues over the phone).

Here's an example. You're speaking to a new client on the phone. His voice is forceful and commanding. He cuts you off if you don't get to the point quickly. He uses words like "bottom line, cut-to-the-chase, get it done, now."

What can this tell you about your client? His language, tone and behavior tell you that he is a no-nonsense, get to the point, always in control type of person. In Face Values language, we call this person GOLD - the Driver.

Using this information, you would know that your communication needs to be succinct and to the point. You better have all your ducks in a row and you better be able to show results, NOW!

Here's an example of face-reading without the face

In a phone discussion about Face Values and People Types, an executive of a Financial Services organization, (let's call him Bud) asked me if I could really tell personality type without giving a written test.

Since I'd never seen Bud before, I asked him to describe the lines in his face. That took five seconds. Then, as a test, I asked if his desk was neatly organized. He paused; that told me that he had to think about it. Then, his verbal answer was, "Uh, it's getting better." Another three seconds.

From an eight-second conversation, I learned enough to tell him that he is a thinker and an intellectual who collects and contemplates information. That he researches his projects to the point of indecision, and he's often late for meetings. Bingo! Bud was amazed at how accurate my assessment was and booked me to speak at the next conference.

Other Facial Elements to Consider

Let's take a few minutes and look at some other facial elements that influence the way we feel about people we meet. Research shows us that certain facial combinations produce a face that people immediately distrust, or trust less than they do other combinations. What facial elements contribute to this?

Here's an example using just eyes (which exert the strongest influence on trust). Which one of the people below would you trust more?

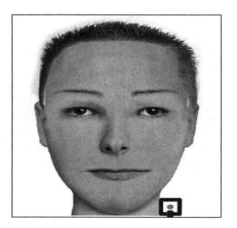 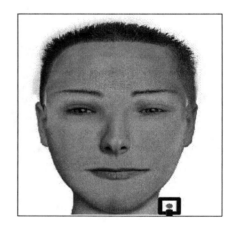

Most people say they trust the person on the left more. The only difference between the two faces is that the one on the left shows eyes that are wide open, while the one on the right has thin slits where the eye is barely viewable. But this subtle fact makes a huge difference when it comes to how we feel about this person and how we act around him.

Although we can't say that a person with thin eyes is shifty or untrustworthy, it is safe to say that people perceive him this way. And after many years, this is bound to have an effect on his personality. The result: He may not be untrustworthy, but chances are he is untrusting.

Let's look at another example.

 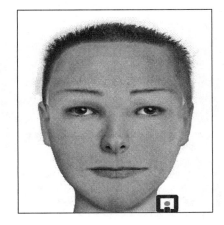

Look at these two faces. You automatically make certain assumptions about each one. We assume one is more gullible and sad, while the other more reserved and skeptical. We also assume the person with the thinner face is smarter. How might these assumptions have affected the personalities of these people through their lives? Are they accurate assumptions?

MORE TO COME: FACE VALUES PART II

– ADDING MENTAL FILTERS

In the second part of *Face Values*, we'll go even deeper into how people think, taking a look at mental filter configuration.

Mental filters are the "switches" inside our minds that determine how we distort, delete and generalize incoming and outgoing information. They are the essential unconscious elements that determine if you'll be outgoing or shy, contemplative or initiating, people-oriented or thing-oriented, a crusader or a defender.

There are about 60 mental filters in our program, but we will focus here on only the ones that we feel are most pertinent to business situations.

We'll also look at combinations of mental filters. After all, Personality Types are simply common clusters of mental filter configurations.

More on this topic in the *Identifying Mental Filters* section of the book.

The Face Values Program

What's Typically Missing

If you've spent much time in the business world or academia, you've probably been introduced to some kind of psychometric survey or personality test. You learned about your Type and – well, that's about it. An hour later, you can't tell what anyone else's Type is. "Uh, I think you're an Expressive Dolphin with a Dominant in your second house." A week later, you might not even remember what your own Type is. Not very effective, is it?

Unfortunately, there is limited value in only learning about your Type. In fact, the greatest value is in learning about those around you and how best to communicate in their language.

The most widely used psychological assessment tool today is the Myers-Briggs Type Indicator (MBTI). Although the MBTI is useful in helping you understand yourself and the people around you, it is not an easy tool to use.

Why? To begin with, there's too much to remember. There are 16 different Personality Type categories. Unless you're working with MBTI on a regular basis, you will forget the classification system. Are you an E or I? An N or S?

What do those letters mean, anyway? If you can't remember your own Type Indicators, it's a safe bet that you won't be able to remember someone else's. Not very effective, is it?

We developed *Face Values* because the other tools we found didn't meet our needs. They required a test, which was impractical in a sales or business situation and they didn't go far enough. The objective is not simply to identify Type but to understand how to deal with, relate to, and build rapport with the other Types in the real world.

That said, *Face Values* is grounded in traditional personality psychology and uses learnings from programs like Myers-Briggs and True Colors.

How Face Values Maps to Other Personality Type Programs

Anyone who's spent any time in Business or Academia has probably been exposed to some sort of personality typing program. We want to use that knowledge – to capitalize on what you already know. Face Values expands that knowledge and more importantly, we show you how to put it to work for you.

Below we've included a matrix showing how Face Values Colors or People Types map to Types in other programs.

Face Values	Gold	Blue	Red	Green
Myers-Briggs	ST	SF	NF	NT
True Colors	Gold	Blue	Orange	Green
Keirsey	Guardian	Idealist	Artisan	Rational
Merrill	Driver	Amiable	Expressive	Analytical
DISC	Dominant	Steadiness	Influencing	Compliant
Hermann	Organize	Personalize	Strategize	Analyze
TIM	Panther	Dolphin	Peacock	Owl
Enneagram	8-Leader	9-Peacemaker	7-Enthusiast	5-Analytical
Hippocrates	Choleric	Phlegmatic	Sanguine	Melancholic
Plato	Guardian	Philosopher	Artisan	Scientist
Spranger	Economic	Religion	Aesthetic	Theoretic

THE FOUR PEOPLE TYPE COLORS

Other Ways to Identify People Types

Before we get into details on the individual types, let's take a quick look at four visual and behavioral areas we can use to recognize the four types (above and beyond what we've learned with facial lines). Remember, the value of this information is that it helps you know how to identify the people type so that you'll know how to communicate with the other person.

1. By Their Office

Green Office

Imagine you're walking down the hall of an office building. You look into each office. When you see one that is wall-to-wall books, half of which are open – that's the Green office.

The Green office usually has stacks and stacks of papers, half-full coffee cups, and the remnants of yesterday's lunch.

When you walk in, the Green will likely continue what they're doing and may not even notice that you're there. They tend to live in their own little world, completely oblivious to what's going on around them.

Blue Office

You can recognize the Blue office by the photos, mementos and the candy dish. Blues love to have people visit and they are always socially accommodating.

When you walk in, the Blue will stop what they're doing, look up at you, smile and immediately start talking – usually about you – making sure you're alright.

Gold Office

The Gold's office is tastefully put together, with everything in it's place. You may find an award or a painting hanging on the wall, and maybe even a nicely framed photo of their spouse or children. What you're not likely to see, however, are mementoes or trinkets or anything that provides real insight into their private lives. Many Golds work every day in an office that looks vacant when they're not sitting at the desk.

When you walk into a Gold's office, he will acknowledge your presence, in a somewhat formal manner. You get the feeling that A) it better be important and B) you better be quick about it.

Red Office

Imagine you're walking down the hall of an office building. You look into each office. When you see one that has walls covered with a mixture of photos, illustrations, articles, post-it notes, cartoons, and phone numbers, that's the Red. Take a seat. Relax. He's probably going to be late.

Once he comes in, the Red will begin talking immediately. He may not give you a chance to say anything. The good news is you'll likely learn something, laugh, or leave with an interesting artifact.

2. On the Phone

Green on the Phone

Greens tend to be methodical and deliberate in their conversation. The pace is often slow, though some Greens talk quite fast. They typically speak in incomplete sentences, and pause often to think or process information. When you're on the phone and can't see them, this can be quite unnerving. "Hello? Are you still there?"

Greens fancy themselves as experts in almost everything, and as such they can be short and sometimes condescending. They disdain small talk or being talked down to. They want information quickly and hate wasting time with details they feel are unimportant.

When you ask a question, Greens sometimes do something very peculiar to their thinking style. As they begin to answer the question, they seem to go to the outer reaches of the universe and work back to earth. Often, they will actually give you an answer to a question you didn't ask. It is an amusing and perplexing trait of their amazing mental prowess.

Blue on the Phone

Blues are friendly and like to chat. They are warm and personable and eager to help. They tend to talk a little slower than Golds or Red, but typically have an upbeat, enthusiastic voice with melodious phrasing.

Because the Blue is so sociable, they can often meander off the subject. It sometimes takes them a long time to get to the point, which can be quite frustrating to the Golds and Greens.

Whether on the phone or in person, the Blue's primary motivator is trust. If they trust you, they will continue the conversation and provide you with whatever information you need. If they don't trust you, then you may as well cut the call short and go on to the next person.

Gold on the Phone

Golds typically talk fast and are very direct. They are articulate, poised and always in control. The quality of the Gold voice is usually forceful and commanding. And, it often sounds like a machine gun or a driver barking out orders.

They don't engage in small talk, and typically will go straight to the bottom line. Of Golds, it is said that they don't have conversations, rather, they conduct class. As you would expect, they like controlling the conversation regardless of the subject or who called whom.

Golds may ask you to do something (such as sending a proposal) before they'll talk to you or they may hand you off to someone else.

Red on the Phone

Reds are expressive, engaging, energetic and easily excitable. Their voices usually are quite distinctive if for no other reason than sheer excitement. They are sociable and love talking, especially about themselves or things about which they are passionate.

In a conversation with a Red, you feel as though you're being sold to, entertained, psychoanalyzed or "saved." It can be both invigorating and exhausting.

Reds are driven by two things – their passions and their need to be liked. If you're not sure whether you're talking to a Red, engage them in a conversation about these two things and listen to the pitch of their voice go up as they get more excited.

3. In a Meeting

Green will either be quiet and aloof, clearly off in their own little world, or they will start talking incessantly, usually about things no one else understands or is interested in. They will also take copious notes and often refer to one of the books or articles they always carry with them.

Blue will be listening intently to the conversation, making sure everyone has coffee and doughnuts, stepping in occasionally to keep the peace. Blues rarely speak their minds in public settings, other than to compliment or build rapport.

Gold will be the voice of structure and reason, but they are more likely to seek control, or at least attempt to control the meeting. So, prepare yourself to deal with a negative response. Golds inherently understand that the person who says, "No" or asks the questions is the most powerful person in the room. They believe in agendas and strict time commitments. Each of those items is a control tool. He who controls the agenda and clock possesses power.

Red will be doodling, singing, pacing – always active. They will participate actively in the conversation, offering all sorts of new and unique ideas that may or may not be related to the topic at hand. They will sometimes withdraw. That happens when they get a big idea and need to work it out in their minds before going manic and blurting it out.

4. Given a Specific Problem to Resolve

Green will go away and think about how to resolve the problem (and probably come back with a matrix). "The fundamental system was flawed, so I developed this work-flow schematic to show..."

Blue will tap into their social network and solicit practical, people-oriented advice for how to solve the problem. "The Boy Scouts might like to be involved."

Red will create a new and better way to approach the problem, including solutions that no one else will have considered. "A charity event, with a blind-folded roller blade race, then we auction off the racers - and of course, conclude with a retro 50s party!"

Gold will form an alliance with other teams, then attempt to take charge of the event. They'll begin assigning work, setting deadlines and managing the team (even if this is not their role).

5. In a Highly Stressful Situation

Greens, who are usually quiet and less emotional, will avoid stressful or emotional situations completely. Like turtles, they pull back into their shells.

Blues, who are usually supportive, tend to acquiesce, rather than add more stress to their lives. Often, they retreat to the point of becoming victims.

Reds, who are usually socially engaging, can attack. Stress for the Red means that options are taken away from them. They feel confined and restricted or pushed into a corner, which sparks a fierce attack.

Golds, who are normally very purposeful in their leadership, become rigid and autocratic. The more stressed they feel, the more they attempt to force control.

INDIVIDUAL PEOPLE TYPES

Now that we've learned about Face Values and People Types on a general level, it's time to take a closer look at each individual Type and see how the facial lines provide insight into how those people's minds work.

You'll notice throughout this next section that we use two terms to describe each Type. One is a general descriptor (Analytical, Expressive, Driver, Amiable) and the second is color (Green, Red, Gold and Blue). They mean the same thing. We use the colors because colors carry no interpretive value. We could just as easily use numbers, but they wouldn't be as visual or as easy to remember.

GREEN - The Analytical

The man in the picture below is thinking. He's working very hard at it. It's his passion. He would rather spend time thinking than doing just about anything in the world. Even though his face may not look like he's enjoying himself, he really is.

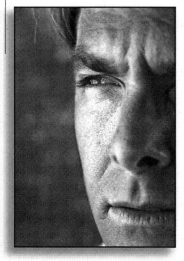

These people are called Green. Other descriptors for this personality type are Analytical, Rational, Compliant, Scientist, and Theoretic.

Greens typically have what we call the "hatchet mark" – one or more small, deep vertical lines between the eyes. The vertical lines are formed when the muscles in the forehead flex, bringing the eyebrows closer together. If you think, contemplate and analyze a lot, these muscles get strong and create the "hatchet mark."

If you don't typically dwell in deep thought for long periods of time, you're probably not using those muscles in the same way and those lines don't develop.

Some Greens also have a "bridge," which is an upside down V between the eyes. The bridge shows that the forehead muscles are being pulled down. When eyebrows come together, they show thinking. When they get pulled down, they show worry.

Someone who has a pronounced bridge might be trapped in a professional or personal relationship where his intellect is not valued (which by the way is the biggest insult and deepest cut to a Green).

Greens Without Lines

One of the most difficult people to read is the Green who doesn't have the thinking line. The face is calm and expressionless, much like the Gold. The way to distinguish between Green and Gold is through the eyes.

Gold's eyes are piercing, and you feel as though they are shooting arrows right into you. There is no question as to where their focus is. The Green's mind is typically someplace else and their eyes reflect this. Even when making eye contact, it's as though they are looking past you and thinking about something else.

The Green's look is sometimes mistaken for sad, while the Gold's is often mistaken for mad.

Greens without the lines between their eyes may have a slightly protruding brow ridge. You'll notice this in the picture of the man shown below.

The Green cannot get enough information or too much time for processing it.

While he is in the act of processing information, he may look like he's frowning or expressing disapproval. Don't be fooled. When he's processing information, he's engaged in the activity he enjoys the most—thinking. Just give him time to finish processing. You don't want to interrupt him, because he is likely to start the process over again (and you'll be there forever).

So you ask a Green a question, pause, and some time later you'll get the answer. You can bet it will be well thought out and delivered with significantly more information than you needed or wanted.

Greens are often slow to make decisions because they recognize that there is always more information that could be gathered and analyzed, and how can you make a good decision with inadequate information?

That said, once a Green makes a decision, you'll have to wait for hell to freeze over before you'll get him to change his mind (so you're better off giving him the time up front).

Greens are individualists who are inwardly focused and have a strong need for freedom and autonomy. They are future-focused and tend to live in both the future and the past, though rarely ever in the present. They may be disassociated, distant and detached from the reality of the moment.

Greens will typically avoid emotional, irrational and volatile situations and are much more comfortable with processes and procedures than they are with people.

Greens have an insatiable appetite for knowledge and a strong need to be right. They are driven to research, rethink, reinvent and redesign. Ask them a question and they will build you a matrix.

Characteristics

Green characteristics include:

- Intellectual and insightful
- Future-focused
- Curious about how things work
- Quality conscious
- A passion for knowing
- Complex problem solver
- Analytical, logical
- Focused
- Likes dealing with new ideas and concepts
- Perfectionist
- Independent
- Objective
- Can't relax and feel comfortable unless they're accomplishing something
- Often appears distant and unemotional

Values

Greens Value:
- Knowledge
- Intelligence
- Learning
- Independence & Autonomy
- Truth
- Peace & Quiet
- Freedom

Relevance in Sales

How do you handle a Green if you're a sales person? Push him with any of the traditional sales tactics, and he'll see it as an attempt to manipulate him. You'll insult his intelligence.

With Greens you have to prove you know what you're talking about. Don't rattle off facts for which you have no data to substantiate. You can count on the Green to call you on it.

If your company is in a competitive market and you don't have a clear advantage, don't try to persuade a Green prospect or client that your product is the best; the research could prove you wrong, and you might never regain your credibility after that.

Instead, it's best to focus on the specific aspects of the product or product design.

Greens appreciate both efficiency and effectiveness. Show how your product is well thought out, thoroughly researched and proven. Show how the design is smart, efficient and effective. Show how it will help them save time or be more effective.

Present information in a structured manner. Most Greens are visual and love charts, graphs and matrices.

Remember what the Green loves to do – think. Show that your product and your personal service will free him and give him more time to do what he does best.

And remember to give her time to think about it. When a Green says I need to think about, she means it. You won't make the sale unless you understand this aspect of their behavior and respect it.

Greens are usually highly intelligent and very proud of their intelligence. One of the worst things you can do is talk down to them or burden them with the petty and inane.

When to Influence

The only time you can really influence a Green's decision making is in the information-gathering stage. Give him high quality information and make sure it meets two Criteria: 1) it's factual; 2) it's not slanted toward your company or product or personal agenda.

Once you provide the information, give him the time he needs to sort through it and make a decision.

Words & Phrases to Use with a Green

Think about what a Green values and use their language when you present to them. Here are same example words and phrases to use with a Green:

- As you know......
- Just think!
- Innovative, state-of-the-art design
- Smart
- Sound
- Well-thought out
- Of course, you'll want to do your own research
- I know you'll want to think about this
- Experts agree...
- It's been through rigorous research and analysis

Summary - Selling to Green

- Make sure you have your facts in order and research to back up what you're saying.
- Be prepared to explain the why and how.
- Deliver information in a structured manner (matrix for example).
- Don't talk down to them or repeat the same information.
- Don't confuse silence for lack of understanding or rejection.
- Allow them time to process the information and do their own research.

Relevance in Management

What does it mean if you're his manager? Just be sure to give Greens important work and lots of time and freedom to gather and process information.

Establish goals and objectives at a high level with Greens and give them autonomy to attack the problem as they see fit. Provide freedom in selecting work assignments and projects and let them chart their progress. Leverage their natural problem solving ability by putting them in situations that utilize these abilities.

Give him the best tools and resources in the department and don't let anyone interrupt him.

If you have a reason to enter his space and discuss something, make sure you don't start with chit chat.

Greens hate wasting time and perceive small talk as a serious waste of their time.

Greens tend to perform tasks in a logical, methodical sequence and they do best when focusing on one thing at a time.

Insulate the Green from administrivia and bureaucratic details. Avoid giving them routine work or imposing stringent deadlines, rules or procedures and don't ask them to share office space with other people.

Greens can be picky about who they work with. They have high standards for themselves and for everyone around them.

Reward Greens with privacy, peace and quiet, meaningful projects, tools that help them do their job more effectively, educational opportunities, or recognition by people they perceive as experts in their field.

Practice: Getting to Know Green

1. Picture one of your clients or coworkers who has the Green's facial marking. List some observations about that person.

   _____
   _____
   _____
   _____

2. Now, does that person's profile remind you of any other people? List them here.

   _____
   _____
   _____
   _____

3. Put a check mark beside the two things out of the list below that Greens value most:

   a. __ Harmony   e. __ Creativity
   b. __ Intelligence   f. __ People
   c. __ Results   g. __ The Bottom Line
   d. __ Information   h. __ Possibilities

4. If you wanted to motivate a Green to take on a project, which one of these phrases would you use?

   a. __ This opportunity will show off your creativity and ability to inspire people. You'll be center stage, you'll have a blast, and the clients will love you!

   b. __ This job calls for an expert, someone who can do the analysis and determine the best process to use to move forward.

   c. __ We need someone to drive this project, to provide the structure and discipline it's been lacking. This is a job for a problem solver and a real go-getter.

   d. __ We need someone that people trust and relate to, someone we can count on to do what's best for the customer and the people on the team.

5. What words would a Green most likely use (i.e. what words should you use to communicate your message to a Green?)

   a. __ Bottom Line
   b. __ Freedom
   c. __ Think about it

d. __ New and innovative
e. __ Options
f. __ Standard operating procedure
g. __ Fun! Wow!
h. __ The old-fashioned way
i. __ Need to know
j. __ Health and well-being
k. __ Proven
l. __ Personal
m. __ Cut to the chase
n. __ Comfort
o. __ Peace-of-mind
p. __ Imagine the possibilities!
q. __ Doing the right thing
r. __ Beautiful
s. __ A real breakthrough
t. __ Common ground
u. __ Famous
v. __ I'm sure you know

6. Invent a T-shirt slogan for Greens:

   _____
   _____
   _____
   _____

7. If you were consoling a Green, what two things would you compliment:

   a. ___ People skills
   b. ___ Intelligence
   c. ___ Accomplishments
   d. ___ Sensitivity
   e. ___ Creativity
   f. ___ Take charge attitude
   g. ___ Vision
   h. ___ Passion

8. What would you *not* say to a Green if you were selling a product or idea:

   a. __ This product was developed by experts and has been fully researched.
   b. __ Most people wouldn't be able to comprehend all the complexities of this product.
   c. __ There's no time for research and analysis. You must make a decision now!
   d. __ We are the recognized experts in this field.
   e. __ Here's how we compare to the competition.

Answer Key for Green:

   3: b and d
   4: b
   5: b, c, d, i, s, v
   7: b and g
   8: c

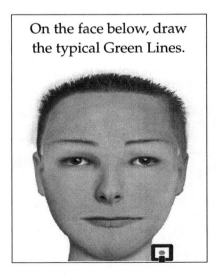

On the face below, draw the typical Green Lines.

NOTES:

BLUE - The Amiable

See the woman in the picture below? See the tilt of her head? That's called the "approachable" posture. People who tilt their heads like that are able to ask questions, then be quiet. They are great listeners. They immediately elicit trust, and they have the ability to get people to talk to them. These people are called Blue.

Pretend you're a guest at a tea party hosted by your four-year-old niece. You can't help but smile at her sweet innocence. What is your face doing? That's probably the signature smiling eyes that tells you what Blue looks like to other people.

Ever hear someone say, "Why am I telling you this?" Chances are that person was talking to a Blue.

Other descriptors for Blues include: Nurturers, Idealists, Amiables, Peacemakers, and Philosopher.

Blues show their Type and values on their faces in the lines next to their eyes. Their "crows feet," "smile lines" or "compassion lines," make them easy to spot.

Those lines start at the outside of the eyes and spread out from there. Such lines indicate someone who smiles from deep within and does it often.

A person who smiles that much looks for relationships, personal connection and peace between people. She is uncomfortable with discord or disharmony.

In fact, comfort is one of her primary psychological drivers. She is a born mediator who avoids conflict and disharmony, working very hard to make sure people understand and respect each other.

Blues are naturals at overcoming distrust and hostility by verbally bonding, touching, or making eye contact. Blues are natural rapport builders.

The Blue's movements are slow and deliberate. Her voice is soft and melodic. She seems to be indecisive because she is slow to judge, basing decisions largely on feelings.

Blues are typically not risk-takers and rarely "go it alone." They are traditional, in-the-box thinkers and prefer structure. They would rather have a "tried and true" solution that other people like them have used, than take a chance on something new and untested.

They are social by nature, though often a bit introverted. They don't like the limelight and seldom get into ego clashes. They rarely take sides and have very little competitive spirit. They are much more comfortable expressing feelings rather than opinions.

Blues almost always think of the well being of others before their own. They are the most helpful, generous and accommodating of all the People Types.

Blues can be easy to spot from the angle of their head in conversation. They're excellent listeners and instinctively cock their head to one side to show accessibility. They also tend to lean their head and shoulders in toward others.

Blues tend to dress for comfort, rather than fashion. They tend toward the conservative and opt for clothes that are durable as well as comfortable. They tend to wear light, pastel colors or rich earth tones.

Blues are typically External, which means they ask other people for advice and opinions on almost everything. Blues tend to trust other people's opinions over their own. In fact, many Blues are comfortable having other people make decisions for them.

Characteristics

Blue characteristics include:

- People oriented
- Patient
- Friendly
- Warm-hearted
- Emphatic
- Sensitive
- Concerned with creating a safe and comfortable environment

- Trustworthy
- Generous
- Sincere
- Cautious
- Team player
- Energy focused outward in the service of others
- Seeks purpose in their lives
- Aesthetic
- Does things slowly and deliberately
- Compassionate

Values

Blues value:

- Family
- Peace & Harmony
- Personal Connections
- Relationships
- Honesty
- Beauty
- Loyalty
- Respect

Relevance to Sales

The Blue values family and personal relationships above all else. They also value animals, the environment and the world (the larger family).

To connect with Blues, you might show that your product or service is good for people, animals and the environment. You should explain that you want a long-term relationship and that you'll personally be there when they need you.

A friend of ours is Public Relations Director for a national chain of bookstores. He deals with obnoxious radio advertising sales people every day. When I was explaining Face Values to him, he challenged me to tell him what I would do to sell radio advertising to him. I looked into his face; saw the blue lines and said:

"John, my company is no better than the quality of my sincerity. With that in mind, I guarantee that you'll be completely taken care of. I'll be your personal go-to contact. In fact, here's my personal cell phone number. You need something, you call me directly. I want your business, but more than that, I want to prove myself to you. And I want to have a long-term relationship with you."

John looked surprised. He said, "Mike, if you talked to me like that, I'd buy your service in a heartbeat!"

You might also show how your product or service will enable them to spend more time with their loved ones since this is a priority for them.

If you say something like, "The bottom line is," or "You need to decide right away," you can go home. You blew it. If you show the slightest lapse in respectability or integrity, you'll dishonor him. And, if you promise a relationship and then don't hold up your end, it's over.

Blues absolutely must trust you in order to do business with you. They want to feel like they know you – that you are part of the family.

One of the biggest benefits you can derive from knowing a Blue is networking. Even if he doesn't buy your product, he'll have an extensive network of people and organizations that need you or your products. So, instead of looking for a sale to a Blue, think about a longer timeline and a larger picture.

A Blue is the perfect strategic alliance partner or advocate for you, but it can only happen if you meet his Criteria.

Words to Use With a Blue

Think about what a Blue values and use their language when you present to them. Example words and phrases include:

- You can trust us to....
- You'll love the....
- Peace of mind
- Family-focused
- Your pace
- Strong relationships
- Sharing
- Comfortable
- Feels good
- The right thing to do
- Stable
- Secure
- Solid
- Grounded
- People-focused
- Harmonious

Summary - Selling to Blue

- Focus on building the relationship first before talking about your product or service
- Slow pace, no pressure approach
- Minimize charts, graphs, technical data
- Provide external references – how other people like them have benefited from your product or service.

Relevance to Management

The Blue is the hub in your office or company. He or she is the person that everyone else goes to when communication, understanding and compassion are important.

Since communication goes both ways, the Blue also represents your key to learning what the "troops" really think.

Blues don't like being the center of attention, the project lead or the "presenter." They are, however, great negotiators, and great behind the scenes support people.

Blues are grounded, practical and represent a good balance to the "blue sky" type thinkers.

Blues prefer structure – an established way of doing things, and occasionally need a bit of prodding. Give them plenty of time to get the job done. Blues approach things slowly and deliberately and they don't like being rushed.

Blues also need reassurance that they are meeting your expectations, that they are appreciated and valued as a part of the team.

Reward Blues with a personal, thoughtful gift, "Thank you," one-on-one praise, reduced workload, or more time off.

Practice: Getting to Know Blue

1. Picture one of your clients or co-workers who has the Blue's facial markings. List some observations about that person.

   _____
   _____
   _____
   _____

2. Now, does that person's profile remind you of any other people? List them here.

   _____
   _____
   _____
   _____

3. The following list contains some values that apply to Blue and some that don't. Put a check mark beside the two things in the list below that Blues value most:

   a. __ Harmony
   b. __ Intelligence
   c. __ Results
   d. __ Information
   e. __ Creativity
   f. __ People
   g. __ The Bottom Line
   h. __ Possibilities

4. If you wanted to motivate a Blue to take on a project, which one of these phrases would you use?

   a. __ This opportunity will show off your creativity and ability to inspire people. You'll be center stage, you'll have a blast, and the clients will love you!

   b. __ This job calls for an expert, someone who can do the analysis and determine the best process to use to move forward.

   c. __ We need someone to drive this project, to provide the structure and discipline it's been lacking. This is a job for a problem solver and a real go-getter.

   d. __ We need someone that people trust and relate to, someone we can count on to do what's best for the customer and the people on the team.

5. What words would a Blue most likely use (i.e. what words should you use to communicate your message to a Blue?)

   a. __ Bottom Line
   b. __ Freedom
   c. __ Think about it
   d. __ New and innovative
   e. __ Options
   f. __ Standard operating procedure
   g. __ Fun! Wow!
   h. __ The old-fashioned way
   i. __ Need to know
   j. __ Health and well-being
   k. __ Proven
   l. __ Personal
   m. __ Cut to the chase
   n. __ Comfort
   o. __ Peace-of-mind
   p. __ Imagine the possibilities!
   q. __ Doing the right thing
   r. __ Beautiful
   s. __ A real breakthrough
   t. __ Common ground
   u. __ Famous
   v. __ I'm sure you know

6. Invent a T-shirt slogan for Blues:

_____

_____

_____

_____

7. If you were consoling a Blue, what two things would you compliment:
   a. ___ People skills
   b. ___ Intelligence
   c. ___ Accomplishments
   d. ___ Sensitivity
   e. ___ Creativity
   f. ___ Take charge attitude
   g. ___ Vision
   h. ___ Passion

People Types 77

8. What would you *not* say to a Blue if you were selling a product or idea:

   a. __ We stand behind our products 100%. Our support team is here for you whenever you need them.

   b. __ Profit potential is enormous, but you must be willing to take a risk and act now.

   c. __ People just like you have been using our products for generations.

   d. __ We are experts in our field. Our track record is excellent.

Answer Key for Blue:

3: a and f

4: d

5: h, j, l, n, o, q, r

7: a and d

8: b

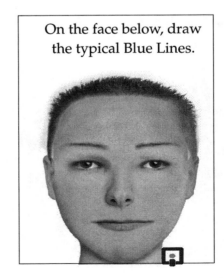

On the face below, draw the typical Blue Lines.

NOTES:

RED - THE EXPRESSIVE

Reds are the people who add life to the things they touch. They are energetic, enthusiastic and fun to be around. The woman in the picture below derives great joy from her creative and physical activities. She is a Red. Other descriptors used to describe her are Creative, Artistic, Expressive, and Aesthetic.

Imagine you are a five-year old opening presents on your birthday. Your eyes are about to pop out of your head with excitement. What is your face doing? Where are your eyebrows? How wide are your eyes?

The Red typically has several horizontal or parallel lines across her forehead that result from raising both her eyebrows in excitement and saying, "Wow!" We call these "Roy Rogers lines."

Think about the faces of Robin Williams or Chris Rock. Is there any question that these people enjoy life, get excited easily and can always be counted on to deliver something unexpected?

On the one hand, Reds have a strong need to be liked and can seem insecure. On the other hand, Reds are bold, self-confident, inspiring, freethinking, fun and intense. One thing's for sure, the Red will always keep you guessing!

In a meeting, they will most likely gesture boldly and expressively with their hands and use their voices like musical instruments. They'll come up with the wildest ideas. Their passion about their ideas is highly contagious.

Reds value creative solutions and crave attention. She tends to act impulsively and she has a short attention span.

Show a Red a spreadsheet and her eyes will probably glaze over. But she'll follow you anywhere if you laugh at her jokes.

She'll be easy to motivate; just compliment her creativity and make her feel as though she's the center of attention.

Reds are the most natural communicators of the four Colors and are typically good at writing, speaking and graphic design. They are also natural networkers, connection-makers, and relationship builders.

Reds are the best of the four colors at "winging it." They are able to think on their feet and are rarely at a loss for words.

Reds take pride in being unpredictable. They have a strong sense of being different and individualistic.

Walking into a Red's office will show you one of the most disorganized environments on the planet. That's because to a Red, organization is a need, not a want, and the Red is driven by wants. She is also probably a visually oriented person. That means she has to see what she's working on. Files can't be in a drawer in a cabinet because they're not in sight.

For Reds this is true: out of sight, out of mind. If you're making a presentation to her, keep everything in plain view and use lots of visuals. Reds also relate well to stories.

On the practical side, Reds will look for creative ways to use established procedures. If she finds something difficult to understand, she'll likely invent an easier way to do it. She'll invent new procedures to improve every system, but she probably won't be able to follow them.

Reds love to bend the rules and hate following rigid procedures.

Expect Reds and Greens to question authority. Reds because rules limit their freedom, and Greens because they think rules are ineffective.

Reds have a tendency to be dramatic and moody with very high highs and very low lows. The good news is, they typically have a positive attitude and don't stay low for long.

Characteristics

Red characteristics include:
- Creative and imaginative
- Quick-witted and humorous
- Good communicator or translator
- Visual
- Kinesthetic
- Able to think on their feet
- Fun loving
- Likes dealing with new ideas and concepts
- Motivates others to enjoy life

- Non-judgmental & open-minded
- Disorganized
- Likes being in the limelight
- Strong need for freedom and variety
- Have a short attention span
- Resilient, great endurance
- Flexible & adaptable
- Rebels against rules
- Likes to stir up the status quo

Values

Reds value:
- Freedom
- Creativity
- Physical Movement
- Connection
- Self-Expression
- Boldness
- Variety
- Relationships
- Fun

Relevance in Sales

Reds are superb communicators. Because most sales and marketing literature is written in "fluff-talk," Reds will be easily irritated and likely to begin editing your brochures.

Making a presentation to them requires you to hold their attention. That's a daunting task, as Reds are easily distracted. They will automatically begin thinking of ways to improve on your performance, or they'll lose interest. Invite them to imagine the possibilities. You might walk them through a guided visualization.

Use visuals and keep the conversation lively. Don't throw out lots of details or data. With Reds, don't worry about an agenda. They're much happier with a more spontaneous approach.

Reds are very action-oriented, so involve them in the process immediately.

Continue to remind them how your product is relevant to them—how it will make them look better, feel better, be better.

Reds value options and flexibility, so be sure to incorporate this into your presentation.

Words to Use With a Red

Think about what a Red values and use their language when you present to them. Here are example words and phrases to use:

- You get plenty of options
- As you can see...
- You can relate
- Freedom to do what you want
- Exciting
- Creative solutions
- Outside-the-box
- Lots of alternatives
- Fun
- You'll be amazed
- Connects to...
- Integrates with...
- Gives you the feeling that...

Summary - Selling to Red

- Use visuals and keep the conversation lively
- Be creative, spontaneous
- Talk about options, flexibility
- Minimize technical details and paperwork
- Compliment their creativity, inventiveness, vision

Relevance in Management

Chances are, the Red employee likes to initiate activities and gets uncomfortable when she's forced into a passive role. So, give her something fun and important to do and provide plenty of freedom and flexibility.

Whether she's interpreting, inventing solutions, or creating alternatives, the Red will always add a different twist. Reds are the classic "out of the box" thinkers. If your firm requires employees to follow specific procedures to the letter – don't hire Reds. If you look for better ways to do things, more effective procedures – more people-oriented solutions, hire Reds and give them the freedom to do what they do best.

You have to give a Red plenty of space. Don't box them in. Reds are uncomfortable with formal structures, particularly the corporate hierarchy. In a perfect job, Reds would float out over all groups, helping out and bringing creative energy wherever they feel they could make a difference. No boundaries, no belonging to a single group or manager, free to roam.

Reds tend to start more things than they finish. As their manager, you'll need to help them be selective about what they're "starting" and provide coaching on how to complete one project or task before starting another.

Be careful to insulate the Red from detailed paperwork and administrivia. They hate it and they're not good at it.

In terms of office space, Reds are happy to share space with others. They work well in group settings, as long as the others in the group are at least moderately social or communicative.

Reward Reds with flexible work hours, creative work spaces, tickets to special events or by implementing their creative ideas.

Practice: Getting to Know Red

1. Picture one of your clients or co-workers who has the Red's facial markings. List some observations about that person.

   _____
   _____
   _____
   _____

2. Now, does that person's profile remind you of any other people? List them here.

   _____
   _____
   _____

3. Put a check mark beside the two things out of the list below that Reds value most:
    a. __ Harmony
    b. __ Intelligence
    c. __ Results
    d. __ Information
    e. __ Creativity
    f. __ People
    g. __ The Bottom Line
    h. __ Possibilities

4. If you wanted to motivate a Red to take on a project, which one of these phrases would you use?
    a. __ This opportunity will show off your creativity and ability to inspire people. You'll be center stage, you'll have a blast, and the clients will love you!
    b. __ This job calls for an expert, someone who can do the analysis and determine the best process to use to move forward.
    c. __ We need someone to drive this project, to provide the structure and discipline it's been lacking. This is a job for a problem solver and a real go-getter.
    d. __ We need someone that people trust and relate to, someone we can count on to do what's best for the customer and the people on the team.

5. What words would a Red most likely use (or what words should you use to communicate your message to a Red?)

a. __ Bottom Line
b. __ Freedom
c. __ Think about it
d. __ New and innovative
e. __ Options
f. __ Standard operating procedure
g. __ Fun! Wow!
h. __ The old-fashioned way
i. __ Need to know
j. __ Health and well being
k. __ Proven
l. __ Personal
m. __ Cut to the chase
n. __ Comfort
o. __ Peace-of-mind
p. __ Imagine the possibilities!
q. __ Doing the right thing
r. __ Beautiful
s. __ A real breakthrough
t. __ Common ground
u. __ Famous
v. __ I'm sure you know

6. Invent a T-shirt slogan for Reds:

   _____
   _____
   _____
   _____

7. If you were consoling a Red, what two things would you compliment:

   a. __ People skills
   b. __ Intelligence
   c. __ Accomplishments
   d. __ Sensitivity
   e. __ Creativity
   f. __ Take-charge attitude
   g. __ Vision
   h. __ Passion

8. What would you not say to a Red if you were selling a product or idea:

   a. __ We stand behind our products 100%. Our support team is here for you whenever you need them.

   b. __ Our products are creative and innovative and we are out-of-the-box thinkers

   c. __ Profit potential is enormous, but you must be willing to take a risk and act now.

   d. __ In order for this to work, you must follow this procedure verbatim.

Answer Key for Reds:

3: e and h

4: a

5: b, d, e, g, l, p, u

7: e and h

8: d

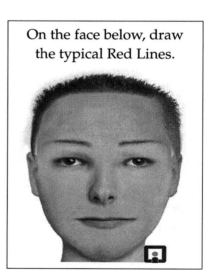

On the face below, draw the typical Red Lines.

GOLD - THE DRIVER

See the woman in the picture below? Would you walk into her office and start chatting about the traffic or the weather? Would you try to engage her in chit-chat as a way to build rapport? No.

She'd call security to escort you out of the building. She is a Gold, and Golds are no-nonsense people who want you to get to the point immediately. They have no time for small talk.

Picture this – you're at the airport to catch a connecting flight on your way to close a million-dollar deal. Checking the computer monitor, you see that your connecting flight is cancelled. You must make some very serious decisions immediately and without much information. What face are you wearing? That's a Gold face.

Other descriptors for this Personality type include Decision-maker, Guardian, Driver, Dominant, Organizer, and Leader.

Golds are the most efficient of the People types and the most likely to adhere to budgets, timetables and procedures. They are highly task-oriented and excellent at follow-through.

The Gold probably has no lines on his forehead. That's because he keeps his emotions at bay, and doesn't show much in the way of expression in his face.

There's plenty going on in the Gold head. However, their faces don't show much (if any) of it. As a result, they have the look of being serious, but calm, cool and collected.

Many Hollywood stars have this profile – Keneau Reeves and William Hurt are examples.

Just look at their foreheads – no lines. That indicates that those people are not actually expressive but are performing in a non-expressive mode. Typically, their roles are one-dimensional.

If that seems contradictory, consider that many character actors don't fit the Gold profile. Picture Jack Nicholson and Gene Hackman. Notice the lines? They're not Gold.

Some Golds show their judging nature in their eyebrows. A person who raises a single eyebrow is a person who probably assesses people, things and situations on a regular basis. In other words, judging comes naturally. The muscles that raise that eyebrow become stronger and more dominant.

Notice the folds of skin above this eyebrow. That's a judging Gold.

A Gold loves comparing value and then making a decision based on it. If you can draw a straight line from initial fact to ultimate decision, you can understand how the Gold focuses his energy. If you can then draw a few lines shooting off to the side, that's where the Gold files anything that's not directly related to the decision-making activity.

The facts – just the facts and give them to me in bullet points!

Golds are action-oriented. They prefer a more traditional approach to things – tried and true, proven, controllable methods. They are not likely to "wing it," improvise or make it up as they go.

If you talk about unproven methods, alternative approaches or "developing markets", you'll upset his sensibilities. That's also a quick way to break any rapport you might have developed.

There are people who have goals - and then there are the Golds. They live and breath goals, deadlines, benchmarks, ROI, supply-chain efficiency and the bottom line. If you can't deliver or operate effectively under that kind of scrutiny, don't try to work with or sell to these people.

Golds are absolutely clear on their goals. They know what they want; they want control; they want results. They can be inflexible, but it's only because they already simplified the puzzle and worked through the logic to arrive at what they feel is the best solution.

As you look at the photos of Gold, think of these people doing all of their expressing inside their heads. They are like machines that have been designed, built and programmed to take in essential information and make quick, calculated decisions based on that information.

Characteristics

Gold characteristics include:

- Action-oriented
- Likes having a plan and following it
- Plays to win
- Responsible
- Sets high standards
- Perfectionist
- Makes decisions easily
- Likes being in charge
- Competitive
- Efficient
- Excels at time management
- Task-oriented
- Focused on immediate and tangible results
- Strong sense of duty and honor
- Learns by doing and bases future actions on experience

Values

Golds Value:
- Success
- Power
- Control
- Commitment
- Duty
- Family
- Loyalty
- Accountability
- Honor
- Right & Wrong
- Tradition
- Practicality

Relevance to Sales

If you're making a presentation to a Gold, always be on time and always dress in classic style. A Gold is not informal. Hedge on the side of understatement. Be sure your numbers are logical and perfect. Be sure to substantiate your claims because this person will gladly shoot holes in them and expose weaknesses you may not have seen.

Get to the bottom line as quickly as possible. Golds are irritated by anything they perceive as wasting their time. They have little tolerance for "how the watch was made" discussions.

Plan ahead what you want to communicate and say it as briefly and to the point as possible. Never deviate or make a short story long. Never improvise.

Golds want to know there is adequate data to back up what you're saying, but they don't want to have to plow through it. Clear and concise summaries with bullet points will win over the Gold.

Golds appreciate a Proactive "get it done" approach. Picture Lee Iacocca and Hillary Rodham Clinton. They are classic Golds. No matter what you think of their decisions or their politics, it's easy to see that those people focus on accomplishing their goals.

In our research for this book, we uncovered a story about Iacocca. When he decided that Chrysler should have a convertible, the engineering department told him it would take nearly a year to build the prototype. Iacocca exclaimed. "Go get a car and saw the top off the damn thing!" That's a perfect Gold focus on getting the job done.

Golds need to be in charge. Respect this when presenting to them. When it's time for you to make a comment, consider what the Gold has said. Elicit his opinion. Show that you respect and appreciate his knowledge and bottom line focus.

Golds are all about accountability so it is critical that you follow through with what you say you're going to do. Never make a promise you can't keep.

Words to Use With Golds

Think about what a Gold values and use their language when you present to them. Here are example words and phrases to use:

- Immediate and tangible results
- You win
- Following your lead
- An eye on the bottom line
- Structured
- Always in control
- Following the plan
- You're in charge
- We get it done
- Producing results
- Responsible
- Accountable
- Cut to the chase
- Take action
- See it through
- The right way
- Succeed
- Impress
- Better than...
- Puts you ahead of.....
- Makes you look good

Summary – Selling to Gold

- Get to the bottom line quickly
- Value their time
- Respect their authority
- Stick to the business at hand
- Do what you promise
- Help them look good
- Ask their opinion

Relevance to Management

Managers need to be very specific about assignments and expectations when dealing with Golds. Golds want to know exactly what is expected of them and the rules or procedures in place for accomplishing the objectives.

Golds are doers. They are good at directly facing an issue or problem head on. In fact, they love solving problems.

Golds look for opportunities to be in control and make decisions. That's why you find so many Golds in management positions.

Golds are highly task oriented and excel at remembering facts and details and creating and following procedures. They take great pride in being right and in doing things right the first time and every time.

They are the most efficient of all the colors, the most accurate and the most likely to complete work on time and under budget. They thrive on accuracy and efficient utilization of time and materials.

The one area where you wouldn't want to put a Gold is in an unstructured, brainstorming situation. Golds are uncomfortable with ambiguity and lack of order. They should participate in creative meetings selectively, to structure them, bring focus, to challenge ideas or to come in after the brainstorming to add practicality and application.

Reward the Gold with increased responsibility, leadership positions, promotion, raise, bonus or award.

Practice: Getting to Know Gold

1. Picture one of your clients or co-workers who has the Gold's facial markings. List some observations about that person.

   _____
   _____
   _____
   _____
   _____

2. Now, does that person's profile remind you of any other people? List them here.

   _____
   _____
   _____
   _____
   _____

3. Put a check mark beside the two things out of the list below that Golds value most:
   a. __ Harmony
   b. __ Intelligence
   c. __ Results
   d. __ Information
   e. __ Creativity
   f. __ People
   g. __ The Bottom Line
   h. __ Possibilities

4. If you wanted to motivate a Gold to take on a project, which one of these phrases would you use?
   a. __ This opportunity will show off your creativity and ability to inspire people. You'll be center stage, you'll have a blast, and the clients will love you!
   b. __ This job calls for an expert, someone who can do the analysis and determine the best process to use to move forward.
   c. __ We need someone to drive this project, to provide the structure and discipline it's been lacking. This is a job for a problem solver and a real go-getter.
   d. __ We need someone that people trust, someone we can count on to do what's best for the customer and the people on the team.

5. What words would a Gold most likely use (or what words should you use to communicate your message to a Gold?)
   a. __ Bottom Line
   b. __ Freedom
   c. __ Think about it
   d. __ New and innovative
   e. __ Options
   f. __ Standard operating procedure
   g. __ Fun! Wow!
   h. __ The old-fashioned way
   i. __ Need to know
   j. __ Health and well-being
   k. __ Proven
   l. __ Personal
   m. __ Cut to the chase
   n. __ Comfort
   o. __ Peace-of-mind
   p. __ Imagine the possibilities!
   q. __ Doing the right thing
   r. __ Beautiful
   s. __ A real breakthrough
   t. __ Common ground
   u. __ Famous
   v. __ I'm sure you know

6. Invent a T-shirt slogan for Golds:

   _____
   _____
   _____
   _____

7. If you were consoling a Gold, what two things would you compliment:
   a. __ People skills
   b. __ Intelligence
   c. __ Accomplishments
   d. __ Sensitivity
   e. __ Creativity
   f. __ Take charge attitude
   g. __ Vision
   h. __ Passion

8. What would you not say to a Gold if you were selling a product or idea:

   a. __ We stand behind our products 100%. Our support team is here for you whenever you need them.

   b. __ We prefer to "make it up as we go." We pride ourselves in our creativity and out-of-the-box thinking.

   c. __ Profit potential is enormous, but you must be willing to take a risk and act now.

   d. __ In order for this to work, you must follow this procedure verbatim.

Answer Key for Gold:

3: c and g

4: c

5: a, f, i, k, m, and u

7: c and f

8: b

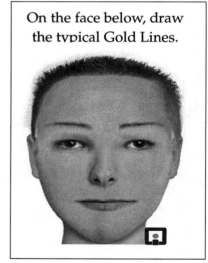

On the face below, draw the typical Gold Lines.

PRACTICE

PRESENTING TO EACH OF THE FOUR TYPES

If an associate of yours were scheduled to make a presentation to each of the four People Types, what would you advise her to do regarding timing, dress, organization of materials, handouts, and conversation?

Fill in the following sections with your answers.

Presenting to Green

Time:_____

_____

_____

_____

Dress:_____

_____

_____

_____

Organization:_____

_____

_____

_____

Practice

Handouts:_____
_____
_____
_____

Conversation:_____
_____
_____
_____

Presenting to Blue

Time:_____
_____
_____
_____

Dress:_____
_____
_____
_____

PRACTICE

Organization: _____
_____
_____
_____

Handouts: _____
_____
_____
_____

Conversation: _____
_____
_____
_____

PRACTICE

Presenting to Red

Time:_____
_____
_____
_____

Dress:_____
_____
_____
_____

Organization:_____
_____
_____
_____

Handouts:_____
_____
_____
_____

Practice

Conversation:_____
_____
_____
_____

Presenting to Gold

Time:_____
_____
_____
_____

Dress:_____
_____
_____
_____

Organization:_____
_____
_____
_____

PRACTICE

Handouts:_____
_____
_____
_____

Conversation:_____
_____
_____
_____

Combinations

People Who are a Blend of Types

Remember these facts:

1. All people possess all four Colors at all times.
2. No one is only one Color.
3. Most people engage one Color consistently.
4. Some people are hybrids – combinations of two Colors.
5. In some people, the combination works well and the person is more effective.
6. In other people, the combination does not work, and he is less effective.

Combinations are like having two people living inside your head. Sometimes they work well together. Other times they generate great tension and stress, rendering the person dysfunctional. In this section you see some of those combinations, and learn what to expect from them.

Gold Green

A common and powerful combination in management is Gold and Green.

The first way you'll recognize them is by the combination of Gold and Green lines or features. This often creates a stern and serious look, as shown in the next photo. Second, they have a forceful, powerful and highly intelligent way of communicating. There is usually no way to out-logic or out-think a person with a Gold Green combination.

History shows us that many powerful people in business possess the combination of Gold and Green. This combination has the ability to analyze loads of information in a flash and make decisions very quickly. They are calm, commanding and very much in control.

These are leaders not followers. We've found the Gold Green combo to be one of the most intimidating combinations on earth. They are strong-willed fighters who seem to be experts in everything. Just ask them.

They tend to be perfectionists and highly critical of both themselves and others. When their emotional health is deficient, they can become dictators. Joseph Stalin is a perfect example of a Gold Green gone wrong.

People with Gold or Green People Types tend to be emotionally detached and distant. When you combine the two, it creates a person who may find it impossible to experience simple intimacy enjoyed by others.

Green Red

If you see both horizontal lines across the forehead and the Green hatchet mark, you could be looking at one of the most deep thinking, creative and driven of all the people types – the Green Red.

He may be a writer or speaker, politician, professor or healer. Whatever profession, this combination of Green and Red is likely to be an out-of-the-box thinker who is highly creative and passionate about his work.

The Green Red seeks to make an impact on the world. However, they're not altruistic; they need to be recognized and liked. People who can manage this intensity possess a balance of thinking and feeling which makes them very effective in a variety of settings. However, in people who can't handle the combination, another life unfolds.

Since the Green tends to be introverted and the Red extroverted, an internal fight ensues, and the person can become dysfunctional. It would look like this. The person gets an amazingly creative idea but:

1) is too introverted to express it.
2) can't express it because the idea is never researched enough and substantiated enough.

Another downside of the Green Red combo is that they tend to take on too much and overestimate what they can do. Hello burnout.

Even in the people who wear this combination well, personal lives can suffer, because people with this much intensity find it difficult to relate to less intense people.

Red Blue

Compassion lines combined with the Roy Rogers lines tells you that you're looking at the quintessential communicator and one of the most amiable and engaging people you'll ever meet.

Red Blues are the consummate people persons. They are personable, emphatic and they love to talk. Half the time, they love to focus on you. Of course, the other half, they focus on themselves.

The Red Blue will sweep you off your feet or at least cause you to think to yourself, "Goodness, what a delightful person!"

Red Blues are natural communicators and people connectors. They are the best of all the color combinations at networking. They're known as advocates and cheerleaders. They often take bold steps in support of an idea or person.

The downside of this combination comes in the form of expressive humor. The Red loves to make people laugh; it's one of the ways he gets approval and becomes liked. The Blue prefers to stay in the background. Picture this, the person talks to you and is so genuine that you melt. Then, he cracks a joke at your expense. If other people laugh, it's all over. The Red comes to life and plays to the audience.

Another downside is self image. The Red Blue has such a need to be liked and in rapport, that he can try to become whatever it takes for the other person to like him. This, of course, is an incongruent identity, and that is a recipe for diminished credibility

Gold Blue

If you see compassion lines around the eyes but few lines anywhere else, you're looking at a loyal, traditional person who is capable of aligning with and inspiring people to accomplish business objectives by demonstrating sincerity and care.

Gold Blues are straight-forward, honest and grounded in reality. They are highly task-oriented and excellent at follow-through. They are industrious and able to manage detailed tasks effectively. They make excellent managers of both people and operations.

The trouble comes when the Gold part, which focuses on efficiency, makes decisions that hurt people. Then, the Blue part, which focuses on people, can get depressed or feel guilty.

Gold Red

If he has the Roy Rogers lines on his forehead, but his eyes show control instead of passion, then you're looking at someone who enjoys power and wears it naturally.

The Gold Red combo produces the ultimate pioneer or inspiring leader – strong and courageous with no shortage of charisma and drive. A balanced Gold Red can be very effective on projects because he is able to see both the big picture and the details.

Like the Green Red combination, the Gold Red combines both thinking and feeling. However, the combination also carries some big trouble. It is often problematic because both sides struggle for the driver's seat.

If there are asymmetrical lines on his forehead (an upside down "V" as shown in the photo below), chances are the person is a perfectionist and the "V" is the sign of disapproval.

Since nothing is ever perfect, the Gold Red feels displeasure and expresses it on his face. This also sends the Red part into a frenzy of discomfort. Reds are not perfectionists and prefer an informal, somewhat chaotic environments. See the problem?

The Gold Red is likely to be continually at war with himself – "It's this way - no it's that way. Take a risk - no play it safe. Here's a new idea - no go with the traditional one."

Both Red and Gold crash under insecurities, and if the Red and Gold parts are not honored, the person becomes a Jekyll and Hyde, at times seeming schizophrenic.

It plays out like this. The Red jumps into alternative solutions and creativity. The Gold pulls and fights for traditional structure.

The Red decides to improvise the presentation, but the Gold needs the structure. Thus, the person bounces back and forth, the presentation is erratic and it fails.

The Gold decides to defer to tradition and the Red explodes out of frustration.

The Gold Red combination of control and creativity is often found in entrepreneurs, as well as the upper ranks of the military and law enforcement.

Blue Green

If you see the vertical lines between the eyes and the smile lines around the eyes, you're looking at a rare and fascinating combination of Blue Green.

Although Blues and Greens typically confound and confuse each other, when you find a balance of both colors in the same person, it can be extremely powerful. You can think of it as intelligence with a heart.

Imagine a balance of thinking and feeling combined with high standards of integrity, an easy-going nature and a tolerant and open-minded attitude.

The Blue Green tends to be very private, slow to act, low-key, stable and fairly predictable.

Problems arise when the person can't find a way to honor both sets of values. The Blue wants to support people and sacrifices intellectual or academic pursuits in the cause of helping people.
The Green, who is totally driven by intellectual or academic pursuits, goes nuts from frustration and begins to feel devalued. Or, the Green side dominates the decisions, excluding people, feelings and intimacy from his life. In either case, feelings of inadequacy and frustration can explode.

Complementary Vs. Combustible Pairings

In the same way some Color combinations are dangerous, putting individuals together can be equally dangerous. The good news is, you can control these combination.

When you're putting together a team, you must match the right types together. When you're matching a sales person to a client, same thing.

This means understanding which color combinations are complementary and which are combustible, then using this information to put people together accordingly.

Here's a quick look:

COMPLIMENTARY	COMBUSTIBLE
GOLD - BLUE	GOLD - RED
GOLD - GREEN	GREEN - BLUE
RED - BLUE	GOLD - GOLD
GREEN - RED	

GOLD AND RED. The most combustible of the color combinations is Gold – Red. That's primarily because these personalities are opposites in so many respects. For example:

GOLDS ARE	REDS ARE
structured	unstructured
by-the-book	anything goes
traditional	creative
organized	disorganized
security focused	risk-taking
sameness	change

The Gold needs to be in control and the Red needs freedom. They are polar opposites. See the problem?

BLUE AND GREEN. There is usually less combustion when you put Greens and Blues together, but only because both colors tend to be introverted (compared to Gold and Red who are both typically extraverted).

In a Green Blue match, however, you'll find great potential for equal amounts of frustration and anxiety.

Greens quickly become annoyed with chit chat or slow moving conversations and they have a powerful need to let people know how smart they are and how much they know. Blues, on the other hand, don't really care about what they know. And, they tend to get their feelings hurt when Greens get intellectually "uppity" with them. They take it personally. Everything to a Blue is personal, while the Green barely even knows what the word "Personal" means. With that tug of war going on internally, the self-talk can get heated.

Once chastised by a Green, a Blue will typically avoid future contact. Greens won't even notice that the Blues are not around. As you can see, this difference in Color can destroy a team that might look perfect on paper.

Combinations that work well, include:

Gold - Blue
&
Green - Red

GOLD AND BLUE. This combination can work well together because they share many of the same values – security, family, doing things right and tradition. They are a good complement to each other because the Blue brings the concern for and care of people that the Gold often loses sight of in the haste to succeed.

GREEN AND RED. This combination can work well together because each has a mutual respect for creativity, innovation, and the quest to build a better mousetrap. They are both visionaries and big-picture thinkers.

Where they differ is how they go about it. Greens are very methodical, Reds are not. Reds are more action-oriented and more social. Greens want to be left alone to work. Remember, the Green is compelled to be the smartest person on the team, so the Red, who needs to be liked, can begin to feel devalued.

When the two understand each other and are able to split up tasks according to strengths, they make a powerful combo.

Putting Your Knowledge to Work

Now that you can read faces and determine personality, what do you do with it? Here are some real life examples of how to put your new knowledge to use.

Imagine that you're making a pitch to a potential client for the first time. There are three decision makers. Person 1 has Red Roy Rogers Lines and Blue smile lines. Person 2 has the Green Hatchet Mark and Person 3 has no lines. How does this flavor your communication?

How do you appeal to all three (actually four) People Types with one presentation?

The Red Blue will primarily focus on relationships and people. She will need to trust you in order for you to make the sale.

The Green and the Gold will need to see facts and figures – proof that you know what you're talking about.

You should get to the point quickly for the Green and Gold, but move slowly enough to build a relationship with the Red Blue.

All three People Types will want to see how what you're selling relates to them – how it will make their lives easier or better. But, these benefits will need to be expressed in different ways.

You'll want to talk about Bottom line for the Gold. Process for the Green. People for the Red Blue. And, you might consider presenting in that order because the Gold is probably the decision maker, while the Green is the decision influencer, and the Red Blue is likely to be the support person.

Exercise 1

Your job is to create a two-person team that will develop alternative strategies for positioning and marketing a new product. This task must be accomplished in a relatively short period of time without ample opportunity to research and test new ideas. Chose the best two people from the four described below.

John: Red, creative, passionate, great ideas, big picture, no attention to detail. Hates being micro-managed, ignores rules and protocol.

Amy: Blue, peacekeeper, easy-going, slow-paced, needs to work around people, detail-oriented, plays by the rules.

Shelly: Gold, hard-driving perfectionist, fast-paced, needs to be in charge, detail-oriented, enforces the rules.

Bill: Green, research focused innovator, analytical, slow-paced, needs to work alone, big-picture, reconfigures the rules.

List 2 possible pairings and why you chose them.

1.

_____

_____

_____

2.
_____
_____
_____
_____
_____

Our "read" on potential pairings

Of the four, John and Bill are the big-picture thinkers and the two most likely to be open to new and alternative ways to do things, so they're the most logical choice, just on these points. But their other characteristics might present problems. Bill needs to work slowly and alone, while John needs to work fast and with people. Are those red flags enough to sabotage the project? Or, could they work together?

Both Amy and Shelly are detail-oriented and value established rules and protocol. That means the project might bog down as they dove into the details. They also might have a problem comfortably operating "outside the box."

John and Shelly both like fast-paced work. But, John would likely resent Shelly's need to control. Shelly would likely have a hard time with John's "fast and loose" approach.

Bill and Shelly may be able to utilize the best of both personalities to accomplish the task. Bill's strategically minded focus and innovative ideas along with Shelly's hard-driving attention to detail may produce a quality product. This pair might work where the task was more technical than creative and people focused. Because this is a marketing and people (i.e. market-focused) task, we suspect Bill and Shelly would not be the best pairing.

Our vote for the best choices are John and Bill.

Exercise 2

Let's say the team you selected worked well and the project was successful. Now, it's your job to select two people to implement the new ideas and strategies created. Who do you select? Why?

_____

_____

Why?

_____

_____

_____

_____

_____

THE FACE VALUES MATRIX

	BLUE *Amiable*	**GOLD** *Driver*
General Characteristics	• Patient • Generous • Cooperative • Genuine • Reliable • Trustworthy • Team player • Ethical • Tactful • Easy going • Warm-hearted • Romantic • Fiercely loyal • Energy focused outward in the service of others • Seeks purpose in their lives • Aesthetic sense • Does things slowly and deliberately • Compassionate	• Responsible • Likes to be in charge • Action oriented • Perfectionist • Sets high standards • Proud • Makes decisions easily • Competitive • Excels at time management • Efficient • Task oriented • Focused on immediate & tangible rather than theory or feelings • Respectful of authority & chain of command • Loyal • Strong sense of duty & honor

GREEN *Analytical*	**RED** *Expressive*	**GENERAL CHARACTERISTICS**
• Intelligent • Curious about how things work • Quality conscious • A passion for knowing • Conceptual, systems thinker • Logical • Strategic • Perfectionist • Work is done, not so much for product or action, but for improvement, perfection, or proof of skill (sheer enjoyment of the process) • Independent • Objective • Complex problem solver • Can't relax & feel comfortable unless they're accomplishing something	• Bold & imaginative • Positive attitude • Kinesthetic • Creative • Needs variety • Introspective & reflective • Improvisational • Spontaneous • Fun loving • Non-judgmental & open-minded • Focuses more on broad concepts than on specific facts • Adventuresome • Risk taking • Resilient; Great endurance • Seeks purpose in their lives • Flexible & adaptable • Inspiring	

	BLUE *Amiable*	**GOLD** *Driver*
Motivated By	Need for personal connection	Power & Control
Values	• Family • Harmony • Honesty • Cooperation • Teamwork • Beauty • Commitment • Loyalty	• Duty • Success • Power • Loyalty • Accountability • Honor • Right & Wrong • Family
Turn Ons	• Pleasant people • Feeling needed • Teaching • Taking care of • Cooperation • Optimism • Kindness • Slow pace • Tranquility • Harmony • Beauty • Security • Order & consistency	• Action • Responsibility • Challenge • Goals • Being in charge • Getting things done • Staying busy • Competition • Winning • Efficient operations • Productivity • Speed • Structured tasks

GREEN *Analytical*	**RED** *Expressive*	**MOTIVATED BY**
Knowledge & Growth	Attention & Freedom	
• Knowledge • Technical Know-How • Mental Capabilities • Freedom • Truth • Wisdom • Justice • World View	• Freedom • Physical Movement • Connection • Self-Expression • Courage • Boldness • Variety • Creativity	**VALUES**
• Learning • Logic • Structure • Challenging problems • Gathering & analyzing data • Applying formulas • Putting things together • Taking things apart • Making things work • Concepts • Questions • Quality	• Freedom • Flexibility • Spontaneity • Imagination • Thinking outside the box • Strategizing • Designing • Integrating • Playing • Lively exchanges of ideas • Crusading • Bringing about change • Moving forward	**TURN ONS**

	BLUE *Amiable*	**GOLD** *Driver*
Turn Ons Cont.	• Sense of family & community • Communication • Relationships • Loyalty / Trust • Teamwork	• Rules & procedures • Predictable outcomes • Public recognition • Tangible rewards • Making money • Leadership roles
Turn Offs	• Conflict • Depression • Rudeness / Tactlessness • Inconsistency • Insincerity • Sudden & frequent change • Loud, aggressive, argumentative people & environments • Hurried pace • Competition • Controversy	• Lack of initiative • Impertinence • Ambiguity • Waste • Chit chat • Confusion • Indecision • Idleness & laziness • Not being prepared • Excuses • Irresponsibility • Slow pace

GREEN *Analytical*	**RED** *Expressive*	
• Opportunity to experiment • Independence • Being "the expert" • Justice • Truth • Serious work • Organization	• Variety • Drama • Taking risks • Having fun • Experimentation • Individuality	**TURN ONS CONT.**
• Incompetence • Pettiness • Injustice • Emotionality • Bureaucracy • Not being productive • Crowds • Chaos / Noise • Lack of focus • Costly shortcuts • Low standards • Disregard for quality	• Rejection • Rigidity • Rules • Authority • Routine • Administrivia • Negativity • Apathy • Waiting • Immobility • Schedules • Tedium	**TURN OFFS**

	BLUE *Amiable*	**GOLD** *Driver*
Decision Making Style	• Cautious • Indecisive (will often delay decisions especially where risk is involved) • Likes other people to make decisions for them	• Makes decisions quickly & confidently, though sometimes without due consideration of the people impact • Likes making decisions for others
Learning Style	• Learns best from watching & working with others • Likes step-by-step, structured instruction • Auditory & kinesthetic • Likes personal stories	• Likes linear, structured, step-by-step processes • Prefers hands-on action over reading about something • Only interested in learning what they have to in order to accomplish the task at hand • Visual & auditory
Ego / Social Style	• Doesn't seek spotlight & seldom gets in ego clashes • Makes everyone feel at ease	• Likes being in charge • Seeks out people of status to associate with • Highly developed social skills

GREEN *Analytical*	**RED** *Expressive*	
• Slow & methodical • Takes in lots of data, likes to do lots of research • Needs time to process	• Likes to stay open till the last minute, but can make decisions easily & quickly when called for • Uses intuition more than facts	**DECISION MAKING STYLE**
• Likes diagrams & models • Prefers to experiment on their own • Likes problem solving exercises • Competency of instruction is extremely important • Visual learner	• Kinesthetic - Learns by doing, by feeling • Visual - Has to see the "big picture" in order to comprehend the details • Prefers interactive programs; discussion • Short attention span, easily bored, often gets off-track	**LEARNING STYLE**
• Quiet, independent & stoic • Unconcerned as to what others think (respects only a chosen few)	• Likes being in the limelight • Relates easily & effortlessly to strangers • Needs to stand out	**EGO / SOCIAL STYLE**

	BLUE *Amiable*	**GOLD** *Driver*
Ego / Social Style Cont.	• Prefers working with others in small groups or one-on-one • Concerned with creating a safe & comfortable social environment	• Comfortable with small or large groups (so long as in command) • Image conscious
Conversational Style	• Often state their point by asking a question • Tend to repeat what others say • Good at small talk • Conversation is more people-oriented than task-oriented • Often touch you while they're talking • Often stop what they're doing to listen • Apologizes frequently	• Can adapt to almost any situation • Always in control • To-the-point • They like controlling the conversation & prefer to do most of the talking • Often ask questions, but don't wait for the answer. Sometimes answer the questions for you

Face Values Matrix

GREEN *Analytical*	**RED** *Expressive*	
• Sometimes comes across as aloof & standoffish • Likes to be alone or with a few close friends	• Prefers to be around people (groups of any size)	EGO / SOCIAL STYLE CONT.
• Asks a lot of questions • Pauses frequently • Tend to talk about things they know a lot about • Like to point our errors or gaps in others' knowledge • Uncomfortable with small talk or emotionality • Often continues working (or doing whatever they were doing) when someone is talking to them	• Tends to talk about themselves • Tells jokes, makes faces • Laughs a lot • Asks intriguing questions • Moves quickly from one topic to another (sometimes in mid-sentence) • Good storyteller • Good listener - motivates others to talk	CONVERSATIONAL STYLE

	BLUE *Amiable*	**GOLD** *Driver*
Demeanor & Gestures	• Comfortable with eye contact • Facially expressive • Slow, gentle gestures, arms and/or palms often open • Easy going, soft-spoken • Leans back in their chair • Nurturing posture • Walks slowly	• Business like • Commanding • Controlled body movements • Erect posture • Some gestures, well placed • Often has vigorously pointing index finger
Sound of the Voice	• Calm & soothing tone • Modulated • Sing-song	• Forceful, parental tone • Very little modulation
Clothes / Appearance	• Practical, traditional look • Soft lines & soft colors - pastels & warm earth tones • Chooses clothes for comfort & utility • Often out of fashion	• Neat, business-like • Prefers a classic look • Cost-conscious • Buys clothes of quality • Takes methodical care of clothing (and all else) • Brand & label conscious • Not a fashion risk-taker

GREEN *Analytical*	**RED** *Expressive*	
• Stoic, unemotional • Quiet & detached • Leans back in the chair • Often has furrowed brow • Walks slowly & deliberately often with head down • Few gestures (except for use of hands to explain)	• Animated • Dramatic • Playful • Energetic • Leans forward in the chair • Moves quickly • Lots of expressions & gestures	**DEMEANOR & GESTURES**
• Calm, quiet • Evenly paced speech with periods of silence for internal processing	• Loud • Animated • Excitable • Fast-paced	**SOUND OF THE VOICE**
• Not particularly fashion savvy • Chooses clothes for comfort & utility • Often wears mismatched pieces • Considers price & durability	• Dramatic - often wears black or bold bright colors • Flair for combining styles, textures & colors • Enjoys creating a unique look	**CLOTHES / APPEARANCE**

	BLUE *Amiable*	**GOLD** *Driver*
Clothes / Appearance Cont.	• Keeps clothes for years, has many sentimental pieces	
When Presenting to Them	• Establish rapport. Start by finding points of agreement or common interest • Emphasize practical applications • Point out the "people" value • Show them how other people like them have benefited from the product or service	• Be punctual & well-prepared • Keep sentences short. Get to the point quickly • Focus on bottom-line impact • Ask their opinion • Influence them early • List advantages & potential problems of proposed plan; have viable alternatives for dealing with what could go wrong • Summarize in writing what is agreed upon
Appeal to	Their personal side	Their pocketbook

GREEN *Analytical*	**RED** *Expressive*	
• Keeps clothes for years (because they can't be bothered to shop)	• Often looks a bit disheveled, but wears it well	**Clothes / Appearance Cont.**
• Present information methodically, step-by-step • Be prepared for requests for details & lots of questions • Make sure your argument is logically sound • Appeal to their sense of fairness • When asking a question, wait (they're processing the information) • Understand / respect their need to be alone to do their own research	• Talk about possibilities & opportunities • Don't focus on details • Keep things moving (they get bored easily) • Establish rapport • Give them a stage & let them perform • Let them know you value their uniqueness • Show them how product or service will benefit them personally	**When Presenting to Them**
Their intellect	Their need for attention	**Appeal to**

	BLUE *Amiable*	**GOLD** *Driver*
Establish Credibility Through	• Personal connection • Focus on values • Show that people they trust use the product or service	• Traditional reports & sources • Focus on the bottom line • Show that the wealthy & successful use it
Words / Phrases to Use	• trust • safety • values • practical • commitment • health & well-being • harmony • security • family • consistent • common ground • share • personally • feels good • fits perfectly with • both practical & beautiful • personalized • protect the ones you love	• bottom line • results • action • respect • precise • complete • efficient • powerful • protect • produce • facts • money-making • low-cost • benefits & privileges include... • makes you look good • good value for money • by the book

Face Values Matrix   143

GREEN *Analytical*	**RED** *Expressive*	
• Facts & figures from respected academic sources • In-depth comparisons & analyses	• Real life stories • Creativity • Vision • Personal Connection	**ESTABLISH CREDIBILITY THROUGH**
• process • model • pattern • map • test • breakthrough • brilliant • ingenious • curious • future • visual • state-of-the-art • system • organic • long-range perspective • truth • scientifically valid • leading edge • completely proven	• unique • bold • imaginative • clever • possibilities • purpose • usability • instinct • Wow! • connections • curious • outside-the-box • dream • passion • feels good • breaking new ground • unique like you • keep the door open • No constraints!	**WORDS / PHRASES TO USE**

	BLUE *Amiable*	**GOLD** *Driver*
Words / Phrases to use Cont.	• simple, straight-foward • nothing hidden • stress free • valuable member of a team • won't produce any arguments • allows you to spend time with your family • built-in simplicity • tried & true • down-to-earth • perfectly sound • safe • secure • the whole family can enjoy • we'll be there with you • peace of mind	• protect what you've built • highly regarded • safe • stood the test of time • willing to do what it takes • gets things done • taking control & keeping it • favorable economic impact • a fraction of the cost • hold onto what's yours • insulate yourself • no-nonsense • fast efficient way to • consistent results • the privileged few
Common Professions	• Nurse • Social Worker • Elementary School Teacher	• Manager / Supervisor • Financial Planner • Stock Broker • Collections Agent

GREEN *Analytical*	RED *Expressive*	
• preferred by the most knowledgeable people • precision quality • the research supports... • well thought out • take all the time you want to make your decision • smart choice • the security of knowing • credible • professional • intellectual elite • finely crafted • the intelligent way to...	• always moving forward • allows you all the freedom you want • stands apart from the pack • time to do what you love • really makes a difference • the choice is yours • now for the first time • there's a world of enjoyment waiting for you • no strings, no BS • now there's a .... made especially for you	**WORDS / PHRASES TO USE CONT.**
• Engineer • Mathematician • Scientist • Neurologist	• Writer • Designer • Publisher • Musician	**COMMON PROFESSIONS**

	BLUE *Amiable*	**GOLD** *Driver*
COMMON PROFESSIONS CONT.	• Veterinarian • Minister • Customer Service Rep • Coach • Counselor • Horticulturist • Florist • Animal Trainer • Flight Attendant • Conference Planner • Politician's wife or assistant • Carpenter • Human Resources Professional • Librarian • Travel Agent • Storekeeper • Dietician / Nutritionist • Cook	• Accountant • Auditor • Athlete • Lawyer • Policeman • Surgeon • Pharmacist • Medical Technician • Real Estate Agent • High School or Vocational School Teacher • Firefighter • School Principal • Mechanic • Proof Reader • Computer Operations • Librarian • Government Employee
BEST APPLICATION OF THEIR TALENT	• Integrating conflicting opinions into a common theme all can support • Customer Support	• Establishing policies, rules & schedules • Ensuring policies, rules & schedules are followed

Face Values Matrix

GREEN *Analytical*	**RED** *Expressive*	
• Designer • Computer Programmer • Strategic Planner • Architect • Composer • Musician • College level Teacher • Philosopher • Psychologist • Gourmet Cook • Forester • FBI Agent • Medical Examiner • Anthropologist • Botanist • Archeologist • Judge • Investment Analyst	• Marketer • Salesman • Artist • Agent • Public Relations Rep • Speaker • Minister • Entertainer • Athlete • Politician • Entrepreneur • Interior Decorator • Restaurateur • Social Worker • Speech Pathologist • Teacher • Psychologist • Conference Planner • Flight Attendant	**COMMON PROFESSIONS CONT.**
• Building conceptual frameworks or systems • Solving complex problems	• Creating • Inspiring & motivating • Communicating • Translating	**BEST APPLICATION OF THEIR TALENT**

	BLUE *Amiable*	**GOLD** *Driver*
Best Application of Their Talent Cont.	• People facing jobs - customer service, counseling, things that involve active listening • Coordinate group activities • Conflict resolution • Teaching, coaching or mentoring	• Solving problems • Fixing things • Where quick decisions have to be made • Highly structured, detail oriented work focused on the bottom line
Interaction	• Allow time for them to "warm up" to you & the people in the group • Avoid implied threats or criticism • Be prepared for spontaneous & open displays of emotion, both positive & negative • Avoid sudden changes in direction or plans • Don't expect big results quickly - they are socially open, but plodders	• Be sure to always deliver on promises & commitments • Carefully evaluate risk situations; if problems, they'll point the finger at you • Expect rigid interpretations of rules; don't ask for compromises or exceptions • Don't misinterpret defense of the status quo as confidence

GREEN *Analytical*	**RED** *Expressive*	
• Developing processes, models, matrices • Long-range planning, strategizing, integration • Research • Diagnoses • Testing • Analysis	• Thinking on their feet. Great in situations that call for unstructured, impromptu solutions • Introducing new concepts • Selling • Entertaining	**Best Application of Their Talent Cont.**
• Don't waste their time with emotional details • Inclined to play the "devil's advocate" & may sometimes use this as a deflection device • Come prepared with lots of information & give them plenty of time to process • Don't confuse what looks like a blank stare with indifference (they're probably just thinking)	• Expect a lot of challenges & criticism • Keep them focused & entertained • Be prepared for spontaneous & open displays of emotion, both positive & negative • Be direct & open in all forms of communication • Let them talk	**Interaction**

	BLUE *Amiable*	**GOLD** *Driver*
Interaction Cont.		• Tend to act defensively, even when a threat isn't present
Work Direction Needed	• Clearly outline expectations in a friendly, but frank way • Make personal contact • Form a relationship • Blues prefers to have the organization define their goals for them	• Give them structured, logical, goal-oriented direction, but room to run things as they see fit • Be precise & clear on expectations & instructions • Give them sufficient & advanced notification of change
Praise Their	• Personal characteristics & contributions • Commitment & participation • Enthusiasm • People skills • Contributions to the well-being & performance of the team	• Thoroughness & sense of responsibility • Caution, carefulness, & accuracy of work • Boldness, bravery, & endurance • Operational performance • Efficiency

Face Values Matrix

GREEN *Analytical*	**RED** *Expressive*	
• When asking a question, wait (they're processing)		**INTERACTION CONT.**
• Communicate concept & give them time & space to process • Don't burden them with insignificant details or administrivia	• Give them plenty of freedom to do it their way • Don't burden them with details • Remind them often of objectives, goals & deadlines	**WORK DIRECTION NEEDED**
• Ideas • Knowledge • Intelligence • Independent initiative • Ingenuity • Logical explanations • Analytical abilities • Value & usefulness of their work	• Creativity • Cleverness • Innovation • Versatility • People skills • Enthusiasm • Perception • Praise them often	**PRAISE THEIR**

	BLUE *Amiable*	**GOLD** *Driver*
Reward With	• Reward their uniqueness & teamwork skills • Give personal recognition • Small, personal ceremonies	• Give them tangible rewards (money, stock, bigger office, promotion) • Advertise their success, new power, etc.
As a Manager	• Sympathetic to personal issues • Makes you feel like you're part of the team • Will do the work for you if you're having a problem • Good coach & mentor • Tends to play mothering "I'll take care of you" role - Gets upset when they feel their "chiildren" are at risk.	• Takes charge & expects to be followed • Confident about how things should be done • Gives orders more often than requests • Lives by the rules & expects you to do the same • Recognizes & rewards efficiency, saving money, productivity • Wants everything in writing • Respects authority & expects you to do the same

GREEN *Analytical*	**RED** *Expressive*	
• Provide sincere recognition but only for significant accomplishments • Reward with contextual rewards–freedom, equipment	• Reward by freeing them to act on their own initiative • Give them a spotlight	**REWARD WITH**
• Visionary • Knowledgeable • Supports training & continuing education • Likely to be "in the trenches" with the troops • Tends to want to stay technical, continue to be an individual contributor • Assumes you know or can figure out what to do (doesn't provide much in the way of guidance)	• Inspiring (Particularly good at inspiring confidence in others) • Forgetful • Works in fits & spurts • Never sure exactly what they think or what they're likely to do (think on their feet) • Will be "in the trenches" with the troops so long as it's entertaining & they feel it serves a purpose • Responds well in a crisis	**AS A MANAGER**

PART II:
IDENTIFYING MENTAL FILTERS

Mental Filters

So far in this journey, you've learned a great deal about people, from simply looking at their faces. If you went no further in this book, you'd already have a tremendous new advantage.

Now, we're going to give you even more. In part two of the journey, we're going to take you even deeper into how minds are wired. In particular, we'll look at mental filters and how our natural mental filtering system works to influence our decisions.

When you learn to recognize how mental filters are configured, you'll be able to predict other people's thinking and behavior.

By the way, the decision-making process is almost always conducted behind the scenes, in the subconscious. The person is normally completely unaware of it.

How we got here

In the ancient days of business, we focused on products. We explained the product features, and if they matched what the buyer was interested in, she bought. A pretty simple and straightforward approach.

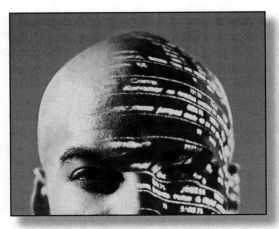

Then, we realized that in order to sell in the new world, we had to sell the way the prospect bought. A mistake was made at that point. The research focused on consumer buying behavior, rather than on the decision-making process. Today, only a few organizations recognize the difference. Lucky for you.

You can't appeal to the way anyone buys until you first discover how that person thinks and what she bases her buying decision on. Pretty simple, but in order to learn how she makes decisions, we need to understand her – get inside her head and understand how she deals with incoming information.

So, the key step in selling and marketing effectively is to identify your best buyers. Then, get inside their heads and find out how each one thinks. Then, make a mental map of that person's mental filter configuration.

On one hand

Remember those sales meetings or appointments when you seemed to do everything perfectly, but in spite of all your efforts, you just couldn't get anything positive from the other person?

Remember those meetings when the other person misinterpreted what you said? Remember those reports you wrote that were criticized to bits even though you said all the right things? How did that happen?

On the other hand

Remember those times when the prospect placed a larger order than you'd expected. Remember when your report was praised throughout the company? How did those things happen? Is it a mystery – or is it just a matter of knowing how to "read" the other person's mind?

This section introduces a simple, easy-to-use, and highly effective mental tool that will make it easy for you to explore the minds of people who are important to you.

The tool has the technical name of a *Language and Behavior Psychometric Methodology*. But, to keep things simple, let's just refer to it as the Language and Behavior (LAB) Profile. Here's what LAB means to you:

1. People with similar behavior patterns have similar language patterns.
2. Observe someone's language patterns and you will be able to predict his behavior.
3. Observe his language patterns and you will be able to influence his behavior.
4. There are about sixty categories of behavior, but we monitor the most important twelve. Here are three things we discover:

    - Does the person look for established procedures to follow or for options to chose from?
    - Does the person initiate activities or prefer to wait and contemplate?
    - Does the person find greater security in things remaining exactly the same, or does she value change and difference?

Those three categories of behavior are vital to increased success with sales and marketing. They tell you how to structure your presentation and what words to use. How's that for important?

You can actually analyze people based on the language patterns they use. And, you can actually influence them by using their own language patterns when communicating back to them.

That was the result of research conducted at MIT in the 1950s by Noam Chomsky. It was then advanced in the 1970s by Richard Bandler and John Grinder.

In 1980, an IBM Researcher and Manager named Rodger Bailey took those concepts and turned them into a simple, easy-to-use tool for defining a person's mental filter configuration.

Bailey developed his tool in the course of creating IBM's internal mentoring program. He knew that in order for students to learn effectively, the student and the mentor had to communicate at a very high level.

Bailey also discovered that this was best accomplished when each person understood how the other person's mental filters are configured.

Rodger Bailey's research and application at IBM resulted in the Language and Behavior Profile. Since its creation, the LAB Profile has been used to improve business at companies like Southwest Airlines, Hewlett-Packard, La Quinta and Pier One.

> Used in conjunction with PeopleTypes and Neuro-linguistic Programming, the Language and Behavior Profile will give you the ability to appear to "read" someone else's mind.

We use it to help our clients attract specific customers and employees. Over time and with much experimentation, we have found the LAB Profile to be a highly effective psychological tool. And, along the way, Rodger Bailey and his wife, Isabel, have become much loved personal friends.

THE ROLE OF CONTEXT

In the majority of personality type programs, you are told: 1) that you have a preferred personality type, 2) that you "ARE" that personality type, and 3) that occasionally, you shift into a different personality type. That would mean sometimes you're Green, and sometimes you might be Blue, Gold or Red. In the real world, that's simply inaccurate. While you might be Green, your "personality" is actually Green plus the Mental Filter configuration for that specific situation or context.

In truth, your "personality" is determined by how you filter incoming information and structure outgoing information in specific contexts. Your behavior tends to be consistent in each context.

In other words, if you're interviewing a job candidate, the context is probably "work." If you're interviewing someone to help her improve business practices, the context might be "business management." If you're having a sales conversation, the context might be "situations related to that product category." The narrower you can get the context, the better information you'll get.

Why is context important? Internal, unconscious strategies for making decisions become habitual early in life. When you discover the strategy for a given context, you know how to get past the filters. And, then, you know how to influence his or her decisions in that context.

What can you learn

When you learn to recognize mental-filter configurations, you can actually explore the mental strategies, values and preferences of bosses, co-workers, family members and clients. You can discover how they filter information, how they make decisions, what influences their decisions, what motivates them, and what confuses them. You can learn how to get closer to someone, and how to repel other people.

Would you want to pick the right strategic alliances and employees? Would you want to find a romantic partner that you would communicate with more easily and with greater understanding?

Would you want to know how to talk with your teen-age children? Communicate better with your spouse?

Making sense of people's mental filters

Picture a big rack of stereo controls, like a graphic equalizer. Each control knob controls a single element like the lowest frequency, or the volume. The knob starts at one extreme and moves all the way to the other extreme. If we're adjusting the tone of the sound, we can turn the bass all the way up.

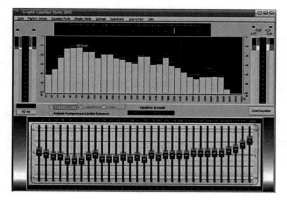

Each bass note in a musical phrase booms like series of explosions and shatters windows.

Then, we can turn the knob and change the sound incrementally, bit-by-bit reducing the bass.

Now, picture another rack of those controls. This time, however, they control different ways you use your mind to filter incoming information.

Face Values focuses on the following eleven mental filters. We'll go through each one and explain what it means to you and how you can use it.

1. Procedures
2. Options
3. Proactive
4. Reactive
5. Sameness
6. Change
7. Toward
8. Away From
9. Internal
10. External
11. Criteria

NOTES:

Procedures and Options

Are you looking for the right way to do things, or alternative ways?

At one extreme of this scale is a mental filter called "Procedures." At the opposite end of the scale is a mental filter called "Options." Most people filter information using mainly one or the other. Very few people use them both equally.

Procedures

Some people prefer (need) to have an established procedure to follow. For illustration, let's assume they fall on the extreme "Procedures" side of the scale. Those people are compelled to follow a procedure when one exists and will typically follow it all the way to the end.

They do not like situations in which they are expected to improvise or "brainstorm." Facing such situations sends them into a sensory overload.

They take offence at the mere thought of breaking the rules. Instead, they believe there is a "right" way to do things. They prefer limited options and very few situations in which they have to make distinctions and choose from a variety of alternatives.

> **Procedures**
> - Follow established procedures
> - Right way to do things
> - Can get stuck if no procedure to follow
> - Compelled to finish a procedure once they start
> - Uncomfortable bending the rules or improvising

People who rely on Procedures are comfortable following rules, but not creating them. Rather than invent new procedures, they will often keep using old ones after they're no longer effective.

A few of the professions that attract people with a preference for procedures include: accounting, auditing, telemarketing, legal compliance, law enforcement, the military, and operations management. IRS agents and safety inspectors are also likely to have a preference for procedures.

OPTIONS

At the opposite extreme from Procedures is a preference for Options. (Remember, this preference is in a specific context.)

For illustration, let's assume they fall on the extreme. As you would expect, these people, are not comfortable with a set way of doing things. When a procedure is imposed on them, they go into a claustrophobic reaction, experiencing a sensory deprivation.

Their preference is to keep their options wide open and "make it up as they go."

People who like Options are innovators. They are compelled to go around the established rules. Interestingly, they can develop new procedures, but won't be able to follow them. Given a surefire method for earning a million dollars, they will change the formula, seeking to "improve" on it.

There is a business philosophy that suggests, "if it ain't broke, break it." Obviously, it was invented by someone who filters for Options. They love to break the rules.

> **Options**
> - Difficultly following procedures
> - Wants to do it in a different way
> - Loves to break or bend the rules
> - Likes to start new projects, though not compelled to finish them

As sales people, if you are not able to recognize the Options orientation, you could be driving a wedge between you and that person from the first Hello.

A few of the professions that attract people with a preference for Options include: advertising, design, research and development, strategic planning, counseling writing, speaking and performing. Entrepreneurs are also more likely to have a preference for Options.

How can you recognize Options & Procedures?

In a formal interview situation, you can ask a specific question

"Why did you choose your <current career>?"

In that question, <current career> represents the context. You could ask, "Why did you choose your current car?" Why did you choose your current financial advisor? Why did you choose your current spouse?

Eventually, if you pay attention, you won't have to ask the question. You will be able to recognize the language pattern in conversation. That's what we do in nearly every conversation of our lives. For now, until you get proficient at recognizing the language patterns, just ask the appropriate question. It always starts the same way:

"Why did you choose...."

Understanding the Answers

There are only two and a half answers to that question. Let's pretend we're talking with Ralph and use this question: "Why did you choose your current financial advisor?"

The first answer is just a list of values Ralph looks for in his advisor. Ralph might say, "I like it that he's a CPA in addition to being a financial guy. He knows the tax laws inside and out. He spends as much time as I need, and his office is convenient."

If you were listening to Ralph's answer, you would take note of these words: CPA, financial guy, tax laws, spends time and convenient.

Those are the things Ralph values, for reasons that are only important to him. All you need to know is that if you or your offering does not meet that Criteria, back out of the deal. If you try to use those values to make a sale, you will be entering dangerous ground and possibly manipulating Ralph in an unethical way.

The second answer is a story. Ralph might say, "My advisor spoke at our neighborhood association in 1998. Then, I saw him again in '99 when I went to a seminar. We got together two times. The first time, we just talked about the market. The second time, we talked about my situation. Next we...."

> IF HE LISTS CRITERIA, HE FILTERS FOR OPTIONS.
>
> IF HE TELLS A STORY, HE FILTERS FOR PROCEDURES.

See the story? Realize that a story is a chronology, and that is a procedure. Events took place in a chronological sequence. That means Ralph defers to procedures.

How can you use this Information?

All people filter information, looking for either Options or Procedures. If you know how Ralph filters it, you can connect with him very effectively. If you don't know, you risk mismatching and killing any chance to help Ralph.

If Ralph Filters for Options

If Ralph filters for Options, you would emphasize that you represent a firm that offers a huge assortment of choices. No limits! Then, you would name them and show how you and your firm matched up with what Ralph values. Remember? CPA, financial guy, tax laws, spends time and convenient.

About 40% of the population filters information for Options, choices and alternatives. With every option you present to them, they'll get a little more excited.

You'd say, "Ralph, our CPA created a list of basic Tax Laws that would affect you. How much time do you have? I'm happy to go over them with you and take as long as we need. In addition, I identified a little-known mutual found that allows you to create your own stock combinations. This way, you and I can build in lots of options, and make changes when you want...."

If you don't include the values Ralph listed, your offering will have no meaning to him. If you didn't structure your presentation in a random fashion, Ralph could have felt trapped instead of jumping into the deal.

If Ralph filters for Procedures

If Ralph filters for Procedures, you would simply explain the steps (procedure) involved in satisfying Ralph. "First we determine what you want to accomplish or protect. Second, we establish how much risk you feel comfortable with. Third we...."

About 40% of the population filters for Procedures. They are suspicious of Options, seeing them as dangerous and a threat to logical order. These people would be on the lookout for rightness. They're compulsive followers of directions and plans. They love time tables, charts and instructions. They will react positively to "step-by-step language."

You'd say, "Ralph, based on years of experience, the program has already been laid out. Just follow this simple procedure. Refer to the outline and the chart and everything will go right, according to plan."

See the procedure? If you don't include the procedure, Ralph will have difficulty following your thoughts. Remember, he subconsciously looks for procedures.

In the financial services industry, the vast majority of advisors filter for Procedures. They make their presentations by giving procedures. But, 40% of the people they talk to are uncomfortable with Procedures. What do you think that does to their sales productivity?

Funny thing. Financial advisors have structured their presentations using Procedures for so long, they don't realize that they're misfiring with 40% of the people they meet. Were they to simply modify their presentations to include some Options language, they would sell more and build more trust.

Sales & Marketing Quick Reference

Procedures:

1. Package your pitch in a series – "First you do this, then this, then this."
2. Get them started in a procedure and they are bound to finish it.
3. Tie your product or service to a tried and true way of doing things.
4. They'll need to know how to buy, so be prepared to provide this information.

5. Influencing Language
    - First then... after which... the last step.
    - Proven methodology
    - Reliable, standardized process
    - As easy as 1-2-3
    - The right way

OPTIONS:

1. Give them plenty of choices.
2. Package your pitch in "choice" language, "There are better ways to find what you are looking for."
3. They'll need to know why they should buy, so be prepared to provide this information.
4. Influencing Language
    - Think of the possibilities
    - Break the rules
    - The sky's the limit
    - Alternatives
    - Freedom to choose
    - Another way

Remember, any of the PeopleTypes can have any of these Mental Filter configurations.

NOTES:

PROACTIVE AND REACTIVE

DO YOU INITIATE ACTION SPONTANEOUSLY OR WAIT AND THINK ABOUT IT?

Walk into any room where people are gathered. Some will be standing and some will be moving around. Some will be seated and leaning back in the chair, while others will be seated leaning forward. Looks like any other roomful of people, right?

What could you possibly determine from just that simple observation? Actually, you can determine who is a "tire kicker" and who is an "impulse buyer." You'll know who wants lots of information and who wants an opportunity to initiate some activity.

Remember, all mental filter configurations can be completely different, depending on the context. Playing Monopoly is a context, and buying an annuity is a different context. Backing up your hard drive is a context, and writing a sales letter is a different context. So, a person could be Reactive in one context and Proactive in another. Look for the behavior in the given situation. Or, listen to the language in the situation.

Mental Filters present you with a two-way street. When you know the language, you can predict the behavior. When you know the behavior, you can predict the language.

PROACTIVE

These are the people leaning forward while sitting, or moving while on their feet. They are comfortable initiating action. They like to move and are uncomfortable with, and possibly offended by inertia. These are Nike's target market – the people you can count on to "just do it". They are not the planners, they are doers. They err to acting first and thinking later. Their unconscious motto is, "Fire, Ready, Aim." Left up to Proactives, all the ammunition would be gone by the time we saw the whites of the enemy's eyes.

Proactive

- Initiates
- Acts with little or no hesitation or consideration
- Fire - Ready- Aim!
- Leans forward
- Constantly moving
- Makes an impact on the world

These people endure lots of criticism for making mistakes, but in the long run, they get things done and accomplish far more than other people.

Proactive people jump into action spontaneously and usually move situations forward without a plan. Their actions may seem disjointed, haphazard and impulsive. Their thinking is that you have to get involved first, then you can adapt and determine how to proceed.

When Proactives are musicians, they improvise. When they are in business, they can waste a lot of time chasing down inefficient ideas. They step into new situations unprepared to succeed. However, when they adapt, they get things done.

Picture yourself on the end of the high diving board at the swimming pool. Do you attempt a dive, no matter how big a belly-flop you might produce? That's Proactive.

In our company, I will often gain a new client or book a speaking engagement, and then figure out how to fulfill the expectations.

Know someone who answers the phone on the first ring? That's probably a Proactive.

Now for some perspective. Pam and I have two dogs that we are devoted to. One day, they got out of the yard. When I realized they were gone, I began running up the street searching for them. About one-hundred yards up the street, I stopped and thought, "What am I doing? I'm letting my tendency to be Proactive work against me." So, I went back to the house and got the car.

REACTIVE

The people leaning back in their chairs are typically the Reactive ones. They are sometimes called "passive or reflective" because in that given situation, they wait for others to lead or initiate the activity.

As you might guess, they are uncomfortable "doing." They typically wait, plan, consider and then take action. Why do they wait? Because they have yet to get enough information to feel comfortable taking action in that context or situation.

Recall a time when you were urged to do something you were uncomfortable with. Take a new job? Break off a relationship? Relocate to another city? You might have protested, saying that you needed more information or more time to consider it. That's an example of being Reactive. Then, once you have gathered the requisite information or waited the requisite length of time, you were able to make the decision and act on it. That's moving from Reactive to Proactive.

Reactive

- Waits for others to initiate action, then follows
- Motivated to wait, analyze, consider and understand
- Ready-Aim – Ready Aim – Ready Aim...
- Leans back
- Relies on luck

Another perspective. Reactives often take criticism for being indecisive. After analyzing them for several years, I believe they are quick to take action, but their goal is to plan for movement – not actually do the movement. So, they're not really indecisive; they simply decide to conduct research and gather data. Then, they take action to develop a strategy. Ultimately, if the data is sound and the strategy valid, they will initiate movement.

Their unconscious motto is, "Ready, aim, re-aim, ready, adjust the sights, ready, aim .... perhaps firing at this point would be premature." Left up to Reactives, the enemy would be having a victory party by the time we finally got around to handing out ammunition!

When Reactives are musicians, they consider spontaneity to be dangerous. Thus, they write out the music before allowing it to be played. When I was a traveling musician (about thirty years ago), I played for a virtuoso guitarist who preferred to rehearse. We went over the material time and time again, *ad nauseum* but never played in public. That's Reactive in the context of playing in public.

Picture yourself on the end of the high diving board at the swimming pool. Do you wait and wait and wait, ultimately maybe going back down the ladder? That's Reactive.

In our business Pam would rather be a guest on Fear Factor than be put in a situation requiring her to improvise. She prefers to have everything perfect first. She gathers massive quantities of relevant information, organizes it into usable subcategories, develops it into strategies, tactics and action items.

Know someone who lets the phone ring several times before answering it? That's probably a Reactive.

Recognizing Proactive & Reactive

1. **Ask**. Just ask any open-ended question that invites the person to talk about how he handled some relevant situation. "What do you do during a typical day at your job?" Or, "Tell me how you handled a recent opportunity or problem." Or, "How do you plan for a vacation?"

2. **Listen to the Language**. A general rule of thumb – the longer and more convoluted the sentence, the greater the likelihood the person is Reactive.

   1. Does the person talk about thinking, contemplating, analyzing, understanding, waiting, planning or luck? Can you see a tendency to avoid action in the descriptions and language? Does he speak in long, rambling, incomplete sentences? Does he convert active verbs into passive verbs by using the "ing" form? If so, that would be a Reactive person.

   2. Does she use short complete sentences and pepper her answer with active verbs like: did, scored, called, made, built, convinced, wrote, created, performed? That's probably a Proactive person.

> REACTIVES
> USE PASSIVE VERBS AND LONG CONVOLUTED SENTENCES.
>
> PROACTIVES
> USE ACTIVE VERBS AND SHORT COMPLETE SENTENCES.

Note: In both of those examples, notice how the language patterns give you a representation of the person's behavior. That's a glimpse of the "two-way street" connecting language and behavior. When you recognize one, you can predict the other.

3. Watch the Body Language. If the person consistently exhibits movement in his posture, he is probably Proactive. So, if seated, he leans forward. If standing, he leans forward or shifts weight often. Is she constantly fidgeting with a pen or spinning a coaster on its edge? She's probably Proactive. There is often some kind of muscular tension, even while listening.

If he consistently leans back in his chair or stands still, he is probably Reactive. Now, remember, that all people will move backward and forward during a conversation or seminar. Look at which one the person is doing over a span of fifteen minutes or more.

Proactive Example. Let's say you ask Mike a question, "How did you get here?" Mike puts his forearms on your desk, leans forward and answers like this: "Jumped in the car and here I am."

In that example, Mike takes action, and the focus of his answer is on himself and his actions. The sentence is short, active and to the point. Proactive people subconsciously impact their world.

Reactive Example. Let's say you ask Eric a question, "How did you get here?" Eric leans back, answers like this: "It was looking like rain, so Weather.com gave me some insight for the, well, you know when it's raining, the interstate tends to be a disaster, but you might have better luck on the loop. So, I thought I could take a chance and come up the turnpike."

In that example, Eric relies on something else to make the decision. He does not impact the world, the focus of his answer is on things outside of himself. He also puts some of his trust in luck, which indicates a lack of personal impact on the world. The sentence is rambling and no action takes place. Reactive people are impacted by the world.

Sales & Marketing Tips for working with Proactive

1. Position your product or service so it appears Proactive or interactive or action-oriented.
2. Use Proactive language with punchy, active verbs and short, active sentences.
3. Link your message to action and movement, inviting people to get involved with it.

Example. In the financial services industry, legal restrictions require marketing material to be written in a language that appeals to Reactive people. So, if you are a financial advisor, your marketing message should contain as many action-oriented words and phrases as legally possible. For example: "Take action today to secure and protect your lifestyle." Or "See the future and seize it now – take the initiative and reinvest your dividends."

Sales & Marketing Tips for working with Reactive

Show how your service gives the Reactive person all the information she needs to become comfortable. Provide the opportunity to wait, learn, think about, and analyze. Facilitate the planning and strategizing.

Example. Entrepreneurs love Proactive people because they buy quickly. The problem is, half the population is more Reactive. So, if you focus on Proactive people, you exclude half your target market. Do this, consider creating a separate letter or brochure, just for Reactive people. Give them greater comfort by making three promises. For example:

1. You'll always get all the information you need to become comfortable with our service.

2. We always clearly clarify and define terminology and elements so you can determine the best strategy.

3. Although stock market fluctuations can quickly affect valuation, we invite you to take all the time you want, and get as comfortable as you like with the information.

PROACTIVE INFLUENCING LANGUAGE

- Get it done
- Jump in
- Initiate
- Make it happen
- Take control
- Decide

REACTIVE INFLUENCING LANGUAGE

- Consider this
- Analyze and understand
- Consider the consequences
- Might, could, should, would
- It happens
- Wait and see
- Plan
- Strategize
- Lucky

NOTES:

Time, Improvement and Change

Let's look at another mental filter and decision factor that all people use. We call it the "Change Filter." There are three settings on this control knob.

1. At one extreme is **Sameness**. The practice of yoga has remained the same for eons. Bookkeeping has remained the same for ages.

2. At the opposite extreme is **Change**. The high-technology industry changes frequently and rapidly. Day traders change the contents of their stock portfolio(s) on a regular bases.

3. And, in the middle, between Sameness and Change is **Progress**. Cosmetic surgery is a business that continually gets smarter and better. It never changes to be different, and it never remains exactly the same. Military weaponry is another example of something that improves constantly.

So, the Change Filter deals with change, and at the same time, it deals with how a person filters for time. Do you seek significant change on a regular basis? Constant, incremental change over a five to seven year period? Or, do you seek things to remain exactly the same through the decades?

When you learn to recognize the Change Filter, you will know:

1. Which people want to make your business a family tradition and which ones see you as a temporary stop.
2. How often clients want to switch products and perhaps what degree of risk they're comfortable with.
3. When a person will probably seek major change.
4. The exact types of words to use in your marketing and sales.

How to Recognize Sameness and Change

Use the questions below to elicit how you filter for time:

1. **Think about eating lunch.**
    a. Do you mainly eat the same thing?
    b. Do you routinely try different things?
    c. Do you mostly eat the same thing and try other dishes from time to time?

2. **Think about your current job.** How long have you been doing the same thing?
    a. 10-15 years
    b. 1 – 3 years
    c. 5 – 7 years

3. **Think about your previous job.** How long did you do that job?
    a. 10-15 years
    b. 1-3 years
    c. 5-7 years

4. **Think about your hobbies or activities.** Do you want them to:
    a. Remain the same with little to no change over many years?
    b. Give you lots of variety and constant change?
    c. Improve steadily over time?

Each of those questions gives you a clear picture of how you filter time. Did you notice that each question also deals with a different context.

Lunch is a context. Your current job is a different context. Your previous job is yet another context. And, your hobbies are still another separate context. Chances are, you don't think about them in exactly the same way.

Now, let's look at the three Change settings and how we would sell to each of them.

SAMENESS

If you selected Option "a" in questions 2 and 3 and have spent 10-15 years doing the same thing in your current job or most recent job, it's a safe bet that you filter time for Sameness.

Sameness people resist change. In fact, they are likely to flatly refuse to change. If you talk about something new and different, you've lost them. They hold tightly to "the way they've always done it." And they continue to do it for 15-25 years. This sameness is their security.

Face Values is a program developed to improve the way people work with and relate to other people. Thus, it will probably not be of much interest to a person who filters for Sameness.

Only 5% of the population has this mental filter pattern. If you want to influence a person with this pattern, you would say:

1. They're the same.
2. Not changed.
3. Exactly as it's always been.
4. See what they have in common.
5. If it ain't broke ...
6. The traditional way

Progress

If you have clients or friends who are self-employed or are entrepreneurs, they probably filter for Progress. They want things to get better at a consistent rate. Then, after five to seven years, they will be ready for some major change. Perhaps they'll move to another city, take a job or sell their company.

Progress people are continually pushing forward. In order to sell *Face Values* to a Progress-oriented person, you'd say:

"*Face Values* is intended for people who want to improve their lives and increase their businesses. It is instrumental in giving them better results with less effort, higher income from more satisfied clients, more personal satisfaction with less stress."

About 73% percent of the population falls into this category. If you want to influence a person with this pattern, you would say:

1. Gets better.
2. Gives you improvement.
3. More (or less)
4. Greater (or lesser)

Difference

If your clients or friends include people who move from one career to another frequently, or jump from one activity to another, they filter for difference in specific categories.

Difference people make up 22% of the population. They like change, so they gravitate toward the new and different. There's a difference to their approach to difference – it doesn't have to be better. Often, just being different is good enough.

If you're a Difference-oriented person, that need for change is harmless when it comes to low-priced consumer items. But, the need can also extend to big-ticket items, like homes, cars, spouses and investments.

If you're a financial advisor, and you recognize that a client filters for Difference, be prepared for a break down in logic. That person will likely look for investments with higher risk, and he'll likely engage in a constant game of buy and sell. The change is more important, even if it means buying high and selling low.

In order to sell *Face Values* to a Difference-oriented person, you'd say:

"This approach to 'reading' people is completely new. And, it combines different approaches in a way that makes it quick to learn and totally unique. What's more, because new material is constantly being added, the program always contains important elements that are new and different."

When you analyze the three responses or sales pitches above, you'll see that we've simply used the appropriate psychological language patterns to match the three basic ways people filter time.

Internal and External

From where do you get your standards: Yourself or someone else?

If you had a control knob that could set the location of where people get their motivation, this would be it. Let's look at an example of how this mental filter plays out in the business world.

Patricia is a corporate attorney. You've presented your information and fielded a stream of insightful questions. She obviously understands the features and benefits. Now, following your sales training, you make your recommendation—tell 'em what to do, right? "My suggestion is for you to buy the Executive Level service. It will do a much better job for you." Then, you sit back, satisfied that she'll concur with your suggestion. Instead, she shows you the door, saying, "I'll think about it." What went wrong?

Your mistake was in making a recommendation instead of saying, "Here are the alternatives; the choice is completely yours ... it's completely up to you. What do you think?" Making a recommendation to someone whose motivation to buy comes from within herself is tantamount to showing disrespect.

Recognizing Internal and External

How can you determine that someone is internally motivated or externally motivated? Just follow this procedure:

1. **Ask,** "Patricia, how do you know if your accountant (housekeeper, butcher, psychic, or other service) is doing a good job?"

   This will show you how Patricia determines value.

2. **Listen** for one of two things – "Someone tells me," or "I can tell." You want to find out if the decision comes from external sources or internal ones.

   > **External**
   > - Need other's people's opinions, outside direction and external feedback to stay motivated
   > - Take information as orders
   > - Are motivated when someone else decides
   > - Have trouble starting or continuing an activity without outside feedback

   You'll know she is External if she answers with: *"The research tells me. The profit and loss statement is all I need. My clients tell me. My boss tells me."* People with this Filter configuration rely on the standards set by someone else. In other words, they are motivated by an External source. If you establish your credibility, that External source could be you. That's why some consultants, advisors and therapists are more successful than others.

You'll know she is Internal if she says: *"I can just tell. I'm good at my job and I know when I've done a good job."* People with the Internal Filter configuration rely primarily on the standards they set for themselves. In other words, they are **Internally** motivated.

Internal

- Provides their own motivation within themselves
- Decide for themselves about the quality of their work
- Gather information from others from outside sources and then decide about it themselves
- Have difficulty accepting criticism
- Take orders as information

If the person indicates valuing other people's opinions, you would cite a list of clients from the same profession, drop a few names or show a page of testimonials. Such a person wants to know what *you* think and will follow *your* advice. You want him or her to be **External** to you.

This reasoning is why expert endorsements work. After all, four out of five doctors can't be wrong.

A person who makes up her own mind, without concern for what anyone else thinks, is at the other end of the spectrum. With her, you would not mention other clients or testimonials.

Simply say, "You're the only one who can make the decision. What do you think?"

Sales & Marketing Tips for working with Externals

1. Externals need to compare their world to an external norm or standard.
2. Provide information on who else has bought the product and how it worked for them.
3. Frame in language of "Experts agree" or "The Research shows..."
4. Externals are more likely to buy when they are told to buy, so be bold – direct them through the decision-making process.
5. Externals are more likely to buy at group presentations and are more likely to buy when others buy.

External Influencing Language

When you communicate with people who get their motivation from external sources, use language like this:

- Experts agree
- It has been approved by...
- I strongly recommend
- Scientific studies show
- References
- You'll get good feedback
- .... thinks

Sales & Marketing Tips for working with Internals

1. Internals are not interested in who else has bought, and they're not interested in your advice.
2. They have their own standards by which they judge a product and make decisions.
3. They may want information but it shouldn't be slanted one way or another. It should be facts and not sales info.
4. Give them the opportunity to make the decision. Don't try to tell them what to do or when to buy. They'll take offense at your pushiness.

Internal Influencing Language

When you communicate with people who get their motivation from within themselves, use language like this:

- Only you can decide
- You might consider
- You'll know what's best
- Call me when you decide
- Here's some information so you can decide
- You know best
- Experts agree

NOTES:

Sort Preference

Do you filter for people, location, activity, knowledge or thing?

Another mental filter we use focuses on what's important. Does the person look at people, location, activity, knowledge or things.

Why is this important? Knowing a person's sort preference gives you valuable information about how to present your information to him.

What a person sorts for ties directly to what he values, providing even more information on how to best relate to him.

Was the D-Day invasion of WWII about the troops involved? Or was it about the strategies and tactics? Was it, perhaps, about the lessons learned? Or even the locations and geography?

Let's first take a look at each of the different sort preferences. Then, we can look at how to recognize each of those sort preferences.

People Sorters

People sorters are most interested in the people in their lives – at home and at work. They will get interested in places, activities, information and things – but only because of the people involved. It's the presence of people that brings meaning to their experiences. In their conversation, you'll hear constant reference to people, including specific names. "I went for a bike ride and ran into Eric, Doug and Anne." Often the people mentioned inside a story become the focus of the story, over-riding everything else.

People sorters sometimes find it hard to leave problem relationships and jobs because of their attachment to the people. Taken to extremes, people-sorters can be codependent and spend their lives solely in the service of others.

Location Sorters

Location sorters are most concerned with where they live, work or visit. They have a strong sense of being connected to the land around them. They see themselves in relation to the environment. Ask them what they remember about a vacation, and they will talk about places, locations, cities and scenic overviews. It's possible that they will mention no people. You might wonder if they were by themselves on the trip.

At the extreme, these people will not relocate, even when staying will mean a drop in their standard of living and moving means an increase in their life style.

Activity Sorters

Activity sorters are most interested in the activities they enjoy. They plan their time around sports, exercise, hobbies and other activities.

They may belong to health clubs, exercise frequently and engage in team or individual sports.

They like being in motion. They can be activists, always going to meetings, rallies and so on.

At the extreme, activity sorters may overexert themselves or engage in dangerous sports.

Knowledge Sorters

Knowledge or Information sorters are most interested in what they can learn about the people, places, activities, and things in their lives. They tend to enjoy bookstores and libraries. They attend courses frequently. They enjoy talking with people who are knowledgeable, not so much for the people but for the connection to their knowledge.

They may plan their vacations and activities to support their need to learn something new. They prefer to live near centers of learning.

At the extreme, these people become professional students and never apply their knowledge.

Things Sorters

People who sort for Things are most interested in what they own or collect – art, cars, homes, clothes and so on. And, they're motivated to acquire more. These are the people who were born to shop. They consider shopping a birthright and thank their lucky stars to live in an age that values catalogs. They are driven to make money so they can acquire more things.

Taken to extremes, these people become "shopaholics." They will charge their credit cards up to the limit and keep them that way. "There's always a new credit card!"

In a business context, a Thing sorter will value systems and process more than people. He may perceive the employees merely as tools in the corporate machine.

How do you recognize sort preference?

You can recognize sort preference in the same way you eventually recognize any of the Mental Filters - by asking open-ended questions, and then listening to the words the person uses. Simply ask someone to describe an event or experience. "Tell me about your vacation. What did you like most about it?" Here's how the different sorting preferences might describe the same European vacation:

People Sorters

"We traveled with the Johnson family, our friends from the neighborhood. We met Jean and Robert Campbell in London. Then, they introduced us to Elizabeth and Edward at the museum. The people were great, and we enjoyed meeting lots of people in each place we visited. My favorite? James, the tour guide and Monty, the bartender."

Location Sorters

"In London we took a cab to the Bradford Hotel near Covent Garden. The next day we went up to Oxford and visited the country home of Inspector Morse. We also went to the tunnels at Liverpool. My favorite? A little pub a block away from Buckingham Palace."

Activity Sorters

"Once we survived the transatlantic flight, we went to a mystery dinner tour in London. It was a treat riding the underground and then crossing the English Channel to attend a wine-tasting event somewhere in France. My favorite? Eating fish and chips while rocking back and forth on that old train."

Knowledge Sorters

"Of course, London is the home of the best museums on earth. And you can't believe the book shops. We collected books on every century of English history. Want to see my map of the London underground? It's a classic example of modernization gone chaotic. My favorite? An obscure book that traces the history of Celtic coins."

Thing Sorters

"We bought some of the most wonderful art pieces. The shopping was magnificent. We were able to pick up some interesting relics. You should have seen the furniture in the hotel we stayed in. My favorite? The china teapot we got from Harrods."

How do you use Sort Preference in Your Sales Presentation?

Earlier in this book, we talked about how to sell to each of the four colors or People Types using their words and their language.

When we talk to a Green, for example, we use phrases like "You know..." "I think..." "Ponder this...." And, if we talk to a Blue, we would mention, "Relationships are important..." "Take care of our family..." "Can I give you a big hug?"

Using Sort Preferences works in much the same way.

People. If a client sorts for People (in a specific context), for example, you'll hear him mention people more than anything else in his conversation. "Mary did this, John did that." Your job is to deliver your information in the same language – the language of people.

Mention specific names, talk about real people – the developers of the product, the people in the company, the customers who love your product.

Activity. If the client sorts for Activity, you would discuss activities with her. Describe the way your firm handles claims or delivers customer service. Use active verbs and punctuate them vocally. You might script out a hypothetical sales pitch and highlight all the verbs. Then, change those verbs into stronger, more action-oriented ones.

Location. For a client who sorts for Location, simply describe your location and the location of your home office. Cite landmarks and show where you are in relation to them. It would be a good idea to have maps handy on which you have already marked the important locations.

Knowledge. People who sort for Knowledge want resource material. They want white papers, research reports, brochures and news clippings. Perhaps the best way to satisfy this person is to give her a copy of your own book. That will immediately establish you as an expert who values knowledge and is happy to share it.

Thing. Clients who sort for Thing have your magnetized business card on their refrigerator. They use pens they picked up at trade shows. They wear logo clothes. So, give your client a pen, a logo T-shirt, a miniature replica of the home office, a lock of the CEO's hair, or any other trinket.

CRITERIA

WHAT IS IMPORTANT TO YOU?

Let's say you're a banker talking to Betty, a 76-year-old great grandmother and widow. You recognize that she has limited money and needs to be concerned about outliving it.

Logically, she's interested in a conservative product that guarantees the safety of her money. You explain to Betty that a certain product is perfect for someone of her age because it represents safety. She says, "Well! If that's all you have for me, then you don't know me very well. Take a hike!" What went wrong?

Your mistake was in assuming that Betty's wants were the same as her needs. You made your recommendation without: 1) getting her to tell you exactly what she wanted, then 2) making sure your offer fit her requirements.

> **Criteria represents the exact reasons Betty or anyone else will buy**

Her requirements are based on her values, or what we call "Criteria," and they represent the most powerful information you can have in just about any selling situation.

Criteria represents the exact reasons Betty or anyone else will buy. Criteria are your link to deeply personal motivators and they are the essence of the elusive "emotional sale." They are just words, but they're attached to memories, attitudes, emotions and experiences. Simply, when you and your product actually match someone's Criteria, you can sell him or her just about anything. Of course, if you or your product prove not to actually match the Criteria, you will have created an adversary.

Note. It's important to make this very serious distinction here. You can make a sale by convincing someone that your product fits that person's Criteria. But, realize that to do so can be unethical and manipulative. Your product must be congruent with what the person actually wants, and your offer must be truthful and honorable.

Until you understand Betty's Criteria, you don't know what motivates her. Where safety appears to be a logical concern, Betty might place a much higher value on setting up an aggressive college education fund for her great grandchildren. You just don't know until you ask. How do you determine Betty's Criteria? Follow this procedure:

1. **Ask,** "What's important to you?"

    If you sell financial products, you know that they affect a person's entire life, so you need to determine what's important to her life.

    Typically, the answers are family, health, freedom, security, achievement and education. Interestingly, "money" is rarely ever on the list. If you sell any other product or service, ask, "What's important to you about (then name your product or service category)."

2. **Ask** a follow-up question, "In terms of (the most appropriate Criteria) what really has to be there for you?"

3. **Be quiet** and listen.

4. **Write** a list of all the things that are important to Betty.

5. **Keep score.** Every time she repeats something, mark it.

6. **Watch** her body language to determine which Criteria are the most important. The more she moves, the more energy is attached to the Criteria being mentioned.

Be precise! Once Betty gives you her Criteria, refer to those words exactly as she said them. Don't paraphrase them. To change them even a little severs the emotional attachment. And, that's as meaningful as giving Christmas gifts on December 28!

To use a word that's different from the ones she gives you is to emasculate the power of the words. That's like going hunting with an unloaded weapon. If she says "protecting me," don't change it to "gives you protection." As similar as they are, those words probably have different meanings to her at an unconscious level.

The Bridge

As soon as Betty gives you her Criteria, ask a follow-up question:

Why is that important to you?

Ask that question no more than three times. You will get two things:

1) more Criteria or verification of other Criteria;
2) you'll discover if Betty wants to include things or exclude them from her life.

Learn more about this vital psychological bridge in the next section.

NOTES:

INCLUSION OR EXCLUSION

ARE YOU LOOKING FOR OPPORTUNITIES OR PROBLEMS TO AVOID?

Remember the control panel of knobs we mentioned earlier? One of those knobs controls your unconscious preference for seeking to include things in your life, or exclude things from your life.

To include something, you move Toward it. To exclude something, you move Away From it.

TOWARD

People who are motivated to move Toward are often considered "driven." They can easily put the past behind them and constantly move toward their goals and objectives. This movement is often made with blind determination. When you see someone with tenacity and perseverance work hard to achieve a goal, that means he moves Toward – in a given context.

People who filter for Toward may not recognize potential problems. What other people would recognize as "red flags," a Toward person might not even see. As a result, Toward people can get into trouble by not adequately assessing risk before implementing ideas.

Toward
- Move Toward a goal or value. Seek to (accomplish, get, achieve, find) what they want or like
- Compelled to focus on the end result
- Often will overlook problems and what can do wrong
- Motivated by goals

Ever meet anyone who was consumed with becoming a professional athlete or artist? Ever meet anyone obsessed with becoming rich? Those people look for information that supports their perception of the world, and they ignore information to the contrary. They see their goal, lock onto it and do whatever they can to accomplish it. Obviously, not all of them have what it takes, so many a driven person burns out and fails to attain the trophy.

Away From

People who want to avoid or exclude something from their lives are motivated to move Away From possible pain and problems. All things being equal, they would rather prevent or resolve a problem than capitalize on a possible opportunity.

Away From people make good problem solvers, auditors, troubleshooters, editors, mechanics and evaluators because they intuitively look for problems to solve and things to fix.

> **Away From**
> - Move Away From (avoid, get rid of, steer clear of) what they don't want or don't like
> - Compelled to "fix" things
> - Focused on problems and what can go wrong
> - Motivated by deadlines

As you would expect, Away From people often miss opportunities by over-analyzing the possible problems associated with them.

Anyone who has ever had a dream knows this scene. You go into a meeting to express the dream. Your hopes and energy are high. However, in the meeting is someone who lists everything that could possibly go wrong. That's an Away From pattern.

If your parents or grandparents lived through the Great Depression, they probably have an Away From pattern in the context of financial security. If you know someone who has lived through some kind of personal trauma, he or she is likely Away From in that context.

Neither Toward nor Away From is the better mental filter to have. Both come with good qualities and not-so good ones, too. In a perfect world, you would want a combination of both.

How can you recognize Toward and Away From?

In a formal interview situation, you can ask a specific question. Obviously you wouldn't ask people whether or not they are Toward or Away From. Instead you'll use more conversational questions like, "Why is xyz important to you?"

For example, you ask Margaret why she lives where she does. If she answers:

> *"It's a safe neighborhood, low crime rate, property taxes are low,"* you'll know that she's Away From. She answers in terms of what she avoids by living where she does – crime and taxes for example.

> If she answers in terms of what she gains – *"We have a huge house in an exclusive neighborhood with great shopping and lots of things to do,"* you'll know she is Toward.

How can you use this information?

Imagine two clients in front of you. One filters for Problems (Away From), the other for Opportunities (Toward). How would you present your services or communicate important information?

Here's an example:

Margaret is Away From, you present your idea to Margaret in Away From language:

- You'll avoid ...
- You'll nip future problems in the bud
- Be ready for unforeseen things that can happen
- You'll be protected from...

Janet is Toward, so you'll present your idea in Toward language:

- You'll gain...get...win
- You'll be able to capitalize on new opportunities
- Take advantage of...
- You'll be able to achieve...

Sales & Marketing Tips for working with Toward

1. They buy because of what they can get or make from the purchase. Show them how this will benefit them.
2. They are typically goal-driven. Show how the product helps them achieve their goals.
3. Minimize discussion of potential problems. Focus on opportunities instead.
4. Influencing Language
   - You get...
   - Your gain
   - Accomplish
   - Benefits include
   - Will enable you to...
   - In line with your goals
   - The advantage of...
   - Opportunity you don't want to miss
   - You can be, do, have...

Sales & Marketing Tips for Working With Away From

1. Likely to buy for what they can avoid because of the purchase (for example, buy investment property to avoid taxes).
2. Package your product in terms of how it prevents, avoids or solves problems.
3. Focus on things that go wrong and how your product responds.
4. Influencing Language
   - You'll avoid...
   - Worry-free
   - Relief from...
   - Get rid of...
   - Safe and secure
   - Protect yourself
   - Prevent ... from happening

Many financial services professionals speak to prospects and clients in terms of return on investment. That is a dangerous practice. Research in decision psychology clearly shows that people are more motivated to avoid loss, rather than seek higher gains.

We urge our financial advisor clients to speak to their clients in both ways. First, cover the Away From points. Then, address the Toward points.

QUESTIONS

As you now know, you can stand in front of most people and learn their People Type(s) simply by looking at the lines of their faces. You also know that when you ask a few questions, you can determine how the person's main Mental Filters are configured. But, what then? How do you find out if what the person tells you is actually what the person believes? The answer, of course, is to ask More Questions!

Why do these questions work?

They give you language patterns containing some very specific insights about how the other person filters information and perceives the world. Once you know those things, all you have to do is present your product or idea in a way that passes through the filters. Remember, this gives you the best chance of making your presentation clear. It won't incite a person to buy a product she doesn't need or want.

Above and Below the Line

When you want to get someone to talk, simply ask "above the line" questions. Those are vague, open-ended questions. When you want to get more detail, simply ask what we call "below the line" questions. Those are specific questions based on information the person has already given you.

Visualize it this way. Picture a ruler standing on end. There's a distinct line right in the middle of the ruler. The top half of the ruler represents the conceptual realm. The questions represented are nonspecific and vague. They are intended to get the person to explore and express.

The bottom half of the ruler represents the concrete realm. The questions represented are specific and seek to get more detail. They ask the person to define in ever smaller bits of data.

Here are some "Above the line" questions:

1. What do you want?
2. How do you know that is what you want?
3. What's important about that goal to you?
4. With whom do you want to share this?
5. What resources do you have to help you achieve your goal?
6. How will getting what you want affect your life?

See how those questions invite internal exploration?

Here are some "Below the line" questions:

1. What is keeping you from getting what you want?
2. How will you know when you get what you want?
3. What will it look like?
4. What will it feel like?
5. How do you know how to get what you want?
6. How do you know that you don't already have it?

See how those questions get the other person to start filling in the gaps and defining specifics?

Tying Mental Filters to Face Value Colors

When we talk about "personality type," we are actually talking about the most common mental filter configurations. That's because personality type is made up of specific mental filter configurations. But, that's a generalized observation. It's not a rule, law or heavenly mandate.

We use both mental filters and Face Values colors to describe a person's thinking and behavior. The Colors concept provides the larger frame in which to view personality. The mental filter components are smaller frames, or more specific characteristics.

Remember, mental filters are contextual, so a person might look for Procedures in one context (for example, talking with a new prospect) and Options in another (driving home in traffic). That said, most people tend to filter information and behave in consistent ways through many (but not all) situations in life.

The following chart shows you how mental filters tie to Face Values colors.

People Type	Mental Filters
Green The Analytical	• Options • Reactive • Progress • Internal • Toward • Knowledge, Activity
Blue The Amiable	• Procedures • Reactive • Sameness • External • Away From • People, Location
Red The Expressive	• Options • Proactive • Change • External • Toward • People, Activity
Gold The Driver	• Procedures • Proactive • Sameness • Internal • Away From • Thing, Activity

As you look through the Matrix, you may realize that many of the people you know fit nicely within it. However, you will also likely think of people who don't exactly fit. That's common. We do too. Simply recognize the person's Face Values color first. Then, see which of the mental filters is off target.

We most often describe people as being a combination of color and mental filters. We'll say, "He's a Gold with an External pattern." Or "She's a Green with Procedures."

There are four basic People Types and about sixty mental filters. If you want, you can get extremely specific in describing how someone thinks and behaves. In this book, we want to give you the basic People Types and the most important mental filters commonly found in business situations.

When you have even an elementary understanding of these concepts, you will find yourself knowing significantly more about the people you meet. You'll see things in them that they don't know about themselves. And, a strange thing will happen to you. Those people you meet will recognize that you are paying attention to them. They will begin to like you more quickly and trust you more easily. It's like pushing over a line of dominoes. One simple push and everything else falls into place, and in a pretty predictable way.

Now, you are better prepared to succeed at a higher level than ever before. You are better prepared to help more people at a higher level. And, you have a greater responsibility.

NOTES:

THE MENTAL FILTERS MATRIX

Mental Filters Matrix

Filter	Description
Toward	These people are energized and motivated to move toward their goals. They are focused on achievement, building, expanding, moving forward. For example: building a successful business or a worry-free retirement.
Away From	These people are energized and motivated to move away from things they perceive as threats or dangers. They are focused on problems or what is going wrong. When motivated, they seek to solve problems, prevent things from happening or remove threats.

Words to Use		Communication Tips
achieve attain can do expand forward goals growth	milestones potential progress push reach towards vision	**Use this language:** • This will get you _____ • The opportunity for you to have _____ • You can reach your goals by _____
avoid careful check crisis danger ensure fix prepared	prevent problem protect ready risk test threat secure	**Use this language:** • This will keep _____ from happening • You can avoid _____ • Protect yourself from _____

Filter	Description
Proactive	This person initiates activity. They act with little hesitation or consideration. They believe it's far better to act than not to act even if it means making a mistake.
Reactive	This person will wait for others to initiate activity, then follow. They need to think and understand before acting. They are motivated to wait, analyze, consider and understand. They feel they are not in control of his or her world. They believe in luck.

Words to Use		Communication Tips
act do go jump	move now seize	**Body Language:** Lean forward, lots of movement, thumbs up, snapping fingers. **Use this language:** • Get going right away • Just do it • Seize the day!
analyze consider could be sure lucky	might think understand wait	**Body Language:** Siting still, thinking, pensive, fist under chin, leaning back, looking down. **Use this language:** • You'll want to think about it • When you feel comfortable with it • It's lucky we're talking now

Filter	Description
INTERNAL	They know within themselves what they want, need, value, trust and believe. They are motivated by their own standards and judgment. They don't need external feedback in order to make a decision. They say, "I" a great deal.
EXTERNAL	They need outside feedback to know how well they are doing or to make an important decision. They often refer to "you." They trust other people for validation and to help them set standards for what is right and appropriate.

Words to Use		Communication Tips
certain confident independent know sure		Always allow them to make the decison. Never try to make it for them. **Use this language:** • As I'm sure you know • Only you can decide • It's up to you • What do you think? • You know what's right
Best practices Common wisdom	guidance support feedback	Provide testimonials, endorsements and stories from people they can relate to. **Use this language:** • Experts agree • So and so says… • Other successful people just like you have chosen…

Filter	Description
OPTIONS	Will bend the rules in pursuit of values. Compelled to seek options and alternatives. Hates having options limited. Feels constrained repeating a procedure. Tends to delay decision making (keeping all the options open). Believes there are many ways of doing things.
PROCEDURES	Prefers a specific well structured process but need help creating them. Believe in the "right way" to do things. May have a compulsive need to finish a procedure once started.

Words to Use		Communication Tips
bend the rules choice creative flexibility freedom innovations	alternatives open option possibility unlimited variety	**Use this language:** • There are lots of choices and options • You get the freedom to choose • I'll create something special for you • There are unlimited possibilities • Search for innovative solutions • Make it up as we go along
according to plan complete the process step-by-step	absolute approved instruction plan procedure right way stable standard	Present in a procedural sequential format and always make sure you complete the procedure. **Use this language:** • From start to finish • First you do this, then this... • It's the right way • Here's how you can _____

About the Authors

Michael Lovas is a Red/Expressive. He's a writer, speaker, teacher and coach. Michael has authored many books, several columns and a thousand articles on Professional Credibility and Psychological Communication. He is the premier practitioner of Psychological Selling for Financial Advisors. You can find him delivering workshops and keynotes throughout the US and Canada.

Pamela Holloway is a Green/Analytical. She's a researcher, program designer, writer and teacher. Pamela is an expert in Human Dynamics - the cultural generational and individual variables that define markets, organizations, and individuals. She delivers keynotes and workshops and writes for several different publications.

Both authors have degrees in Psychology, augmented with extensive post graduate work in Neuro-linguistic Programming (NLP). Michael is also a certified Trainer of NLP and a Clinical Hypnotherapist.

Lovas and Holloway funnel their passions into the firm they founded - AboutPeople, a unique consultancy focused on helping companies and individuals better understand, attract and connect with their target audiences.

Lovas and Holloway are married and live in Spokane Washington.